TALES FROM THE TOMBSTONE:

MISDEEDS & MURDER

BY S BALLINGER & P COOMBES

Dedicated to all the members of the Tales from the
Tombstone group

TABLE OF CONTENTS

ACKNOWLEDGEMENTS

We would like to thank the following people, writer A.J Griffiths Jones for finding the newspaper reports on Florence Porter, Darren Gibbs for the title of the book and a big thank you to David Hall for his time and patience as a proof-reader for this book.

INTRODUCTION

All of the following are true stories (1600-1954) that were discovered while working on other projects.

Where possible we have added documents, newspaper cuttings and photos to accompany the stories.

Please be aware some of the stories that appear in this book appear in our other books; 'Tales from the Tombstone' and 'Buried Past: Tales from a Cheltenham Cemetery', while others are completely new and have not appeared in any of the books.

Also please be aware we are not professional historians or writers. The main contributor to the writing is dyslexic and mistakes may be found for which we apologise.

UNCONVENTIONAL LAWS

When the Waltham Black Act of 1723, (commonly known as the Bloody Code) was established in Britain, it imposed the death penalty for over 200 offences, many of which were trivial.

Some of the offences were as follows:

Burglary
murder
arson
forgery
cutting down trees
stealing horses or sheep
destroying turnpike roads
pickpocketing goods worth a shilling
being out at night with a blackened face
being an unmarried mother concealing a stillborn child

Many juries and judges were reluctant to find people guilty of petty crimes; instead, they would acquit a criminal rather than give the death penalty. Others however would use transportation as a less harsh punishment, but one that would still deter people from crime. Therefore in practice, the death penalty as a deterrent for so many crimes, did not work.

This brings us to the case of the last woman hanged in Gloucestershire for Arson: Charlotte Long.

Charlotte Long was born Charlotte Bendall in 1799 to Thomas and Sarah Bendall of North Nibley,

Gloucestershire. On 10 March 1819, she married John Long, and the couple had two children, George and Elizabeth.

In 1829, at the Gloucester Assizes, John Long was convicted of stealing bacon and sentenced to be transported to Australia for seven years, leaving Charlotte alone with the children.

In April 1833, Charlotte, by now 33 years old, was once again pregnant and, obviously, the father was not her husband John. She was therefore removed from North Nibley by parish officer, Henry Excell, because she would be a financial burden on the parish. However, in July of the same year, she had returned to North Nibley, now with a third child; a son called William.

On the night of 25 July 1833, in North Nibley, the hay-ricks of three farmers, Jesse Organ, Thomas Gilman and James Nicholls were set on fire. Each blaze was quickly extinguished and no great damage was done, but it was suspected that an arsonist had been at work. The culprit was soon detained when a woman called Betsey Burford came forward and accused Charlotte Long of being the arsonist.

Henry Excell in his position as parish officer obtained an arrest warrant for Charlotte. On arrival at her home, he arrested her on the charge of setting fire to the hay-ricks. Charlotte asked who had named her, and Excell told her that Betsey Burford had sworn that Charlotte was responsible for causing the fires.

She replied, "Betsey Burford has dug a ditch for me, and I shall fall into it" and protested that Burford had encouraged her to commit the crime.

Charlotte was admitted to Gloucester Gaol on 9th August where she was placed in the care of Mrs Linton, one of the matrons at the prison. Charlotte confessed to Mrs Linton that she had set fire to the ricks and told her that she hoped God would forgive her. She again implicated Betsey Burford.

Now it was Betsey Burford's turn to be arrested and charged with aiding and abetting Charlotte, but to save herself, she gave evidence against Charlotte.

Charlotte came to trial at the Gloucester Summer Assizes on Friday 23 August 1833, before Baron Gurney. In court, Betsey Burford testified that Charlotte had decided to set fire to the hayricks belonging to Henry Excell in revenge for removing her from North Nibley, but refrained from doing so at the last minute because she would be the prime suspect. Other witnesses gave evidence of seeing a woman who looked like Charlotte, hurrying away from the crime scene. Baron Gurney questioned them as to whether the woman they had seen was limping; they answered that she was not. This was important because Betsey Burford walked with a limp, whilst Charlotte didn't.

With evidence weighing heavily against Charlotte, she was found guilty and sentenced to hang.

Both Jesse Organ, one of the farmers whose hay-ricks were destroyed, and the jury made a strong recommendation for mercy, but Baron Gurney rejected this.

In the condemned cell, Charlotte confessed to her crime saying that she had set fire to the hayricks belonging to the three farmers to divert attention away from her when she set fire to those belonging to Henry Excell. She continued to insist that Betsey Burford had persuaded her to commit the crime and had instructed her on how to set the fires. She also suggested that Betsey had offered her money to do so.

Charlotte Long's son William who was in the care of his aunt, died before the sentence was carried out. When Charlotte was told that her child had died; she replied she was glad because she would see him soon in heaven.

Charlotte was hanged side by side with Thomas Gaskins who was convicted of arson, at Gloucester Gaol just after 11 am on Saturday 31st August, before a large crowd of spectators.

As Charlotte had not been convicted of murder, she was granted burial in the churchyard of St Martin's Parish Church North Nibley, on 3 September 1833; in the same church where she was baptised and married.

Charlotte Long was the last woman to be hanged in England for committing arson. The last man to be hanged in England for the same offence was Daniel Chase, who died at Ilchester, Somerset, on 31 August 1836.

in the County of *Gloucester*		in the Year 18_35_		
Name.	Abode.	When buried.	Age.	By whom the Ceremony was performed.
William Webb No. 441.	Nibley	Sept. 1.	6	W. H. Thompson Curate
Executed at Gloucester Charlotte Long for Arson Aug. 31st No. 442.	Nibley	Sept. 3.	33	W. H. Thompson Curate

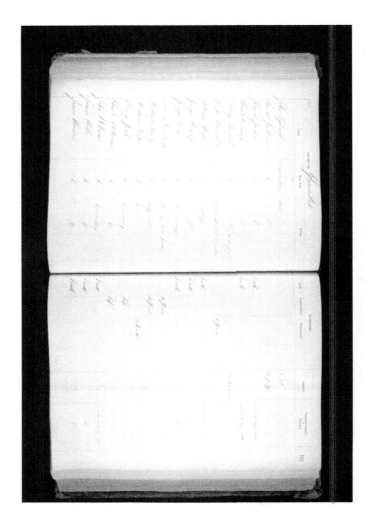

Charlotte Long's Prison Record

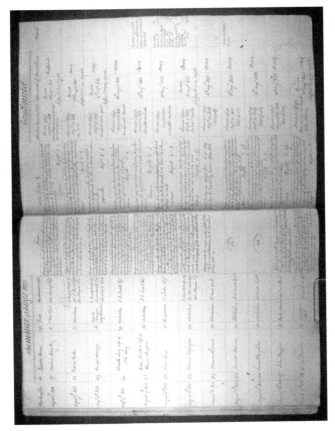

Charlotte Long's Prison Record

As we mentioned in the previous story, Charlotte didn't hang alone. Beside her was Thomas Gaskins of Deerhurst, Tewkesbury, age 26.

His crime was also one of 'arson of hayricks', belonging to his master John Lane. It would appear John held no ill will towards Thomas and described him as honest and hardworking. This was Thomas's first offence and he was intoxicated at the time of the offence, but like Charlotte, nothing could save him.

His brother Samuel was also indicted but was acquitted of being an accessory after the fact.

Thomas's body was returned to his family and he was buried in Deerhurst.

In 1837 most forms of arson were removed from the list of capital offences

---

At the Gloucester Assizes, on Friday week, Charlotte Long was found guilty of setting fire to three ricks of hay, at North Nibley, in Gloucestershire, on the 25th July last. She was recommended to mercy by the Jury, on the ground that she had probably been instigated to commit the offence by some other person. Baron Gurney said that he could not attend to their recommendation; the prisoner was the wife of a convicted felon, and had set fire to three different ricks of hay; and although it was not improbable that she had been instigated to the deed by some other person, yet there would be no security for property, if the penalty of the law were remitted in this instance.

At the same time that this woman was condemned, Thomas Gaskins, who had been convicted of arson the day before, was also sentenced to be hanged. The man shed tears, but the cries and shrieks of the woman were shocking.

The Cambrian 24 August 1833

Gloucester Assizes terminated on Friday evening. Out of nearly 100 prisoners which the calendar contained, two were condemned and left for execution, viz. *Thomas Gaskins* and *Charlotte Long*, both convicted upon the clearest evidence, of arson, in setting fire to ricks, the former at Deerhurst, and the latter at North Nibley. In both instances the prisoners were recommended to mercy by the prosecutors and jury, but the Learned Judge in passing sentence, observed, with evident distress of mind, that a painful and insurmountable sense of what was due to society compelled him to leave the culprits to their fate without the slightest hope of mercy being extended to them. The very impressive terms in which the sentence was delivered made a sensible impression upon a crowded court, which was still more increased by the anguish of the female prisoner, who, when first placed at the bar, had an infant only a few weeks old, at the breast. The cases at *Nisi Prius* were 34 in number, but, with the exception of the following, none possessed any interest but to the parties concerned :—

Burial Record for Thomas Gaskins with an additional note saying he was executed for arson.

According to the records in Gloucestershire during the years 1805-1833, 60 criminals were executed; of these

15 for attempted murder or murder
13 for burglary
26 for robbery, shooting, horse and sheep theft
1 for forgery
1 for rape
1 for Arson
3 for housebreaking

Of those executed for housebreaking was a 69-year-old woman called Dinah Riddiford from Thornbury.

On 30 July 1816, four members of the Riddiford family from Thornbury were committed to Gloucester Gaol. They were Abraham Riddiford, his wife Dinah, 63, with their sons Luke and Aaron.

The charges against them were breaking into the home of Daniel Reed, and stealing two sides of bacon, two pig cheeks, a tongue piece, two sweet bones, 30lb of salt butter, and lastly a copper kettle amounting to about 4 pounds worth of goods.

Dinah and her son Luke were condemned to death by hanging; a very harsh punishment for stealing bacon and butter, whilst her husband and Aaron were acquitted.

Luke's sentence was later commuted to transportation for life, but Dinah received no reprieve.

On 6th September just before her execution, Dinah made a full confession to her part in the crime. She was the last woman to die for a conventional property offence.

Her body was returned to Thornbury and buried within the grounds of St Mary's church, on 10 September 1816.

Dinah Riddiford was probably the oldest woman hanged in the 19th century for housebreaking.

In December 1816, Luke Riddiford was placed on the prison ship, Justia, which was docked in the Thames, at Woolwich, London. On 11 April 1817, he was transported to the prison ship, Lord Eldon, which arrived at Port Jackson Sydney, on 30 September 1817.

With a bit of research, we found that the following year, on 18 March 1818, Luke was listed as an escaped convict, and it would appear he stayed at large until August 18 1821, when he was charged with robbing and assaulting a man, for which he received 100 lashes. Subsequently, we do not know what happened to Riddiford after this.

Abraham Riddiford

Luke Riddiford

Dinah Riddiford

Aaron Riddiford

charged upon the oath of Daniel Reed of Thornbury cordwainer with feloniously taking stealing and carrying away in the night time from his dwelling house two sides of bacon two hogs cheeks, one tongue piece two sweetbones one copper teakettle and about 36 lb of salt butter in an earthen pan of the value of £4 the property of him the said Daniel Reed

Burial Record for Dinah Riddiford

Page 15.

BURIALS in the Parish of _Thornbury_
in the County of _Gloucester_ in the Year 1820

Name.	Abode.	When buried.	Age.	By whom the Ceremony was performed.
Robert Knight No. 113.	Thornbury	July 14th	Infant	M. Terry
Elizabeth Young No. 114.	Northwood part of Weston on Toynt	August 7th	37	R. Slade
Thomas Barton No. 115.	Brinkmarsh in Moreton	August 19th	38	M. Terry
Dinah Riddiford No. 116.	Thornbury	Sept 10th	68	R. Slade

Luke Riddiford Ship Record

PETTY TREASON

If a woman killed her husband, she was not just guilty of murder, but the more serious crime of Petty Treason.

Petty Treason was defined by the Treason Act of 1351 as a wife killing her husband, a clergyman killing a high-ranking member of the clergy such as a Bishop or an Abbot, a servant killing his master or mistress, or his master's wife.

However, this law did not apply to a husband who murdered his wife. In many cases, the husband was charged with manslaughter using the defence of provocation by his wife.

Women convicted of petty treason and high treason could be burned at the stake until 1793, and at least 32 women suffered this fate between 1735 and 1789. Two women convicted under the Petty Treason Act, were Anne Williams and Susannah Bruford; both were sentenced to burn at the stake in 1753 for the murder of their husbands.

The following is the story of Anne Williams.

In June 1752, Anne Williams was admitted to Cirencester House of Correction, on suspicion of poisoning her husband, William Williams.

The family of Anne Williams, described her as a terrible and argumentative woman; her husband William Williams was the reverse, he was described as a mild-mannered and even-tempered man; his only fault being to put up with Anne's abusive and violent behaviour towards him.

In June of 1752, Anne decided enough was enough and plotted to murder him. Anne's first action was to persuade the couple's servant, Richard Painter, to purchase some white mercury. This was easily accomplished. She then mixed the mercury into some gruel and made her husband eat it, which added insult to injury as her husband did not like gruel. Anne also made her husband drink ale, presumably laced with mercury. Not long after, William was taken ill, seized with violent vomiting. The dying husband sent for his sister, telling her his wife was a wicked woman, and that he felt well until being forced to eat some pap. Despite medical aid, he died the next day.

Arrested and charged under the law of Petty Treason, Anne had to wait until April of the following year for her trial to take place at the Lent Assizes. She was found guilty and sentenced to be burnt at the stake, which was accordingly carried out in Over, near Gloucester, on April 13 1753, (incidentally a Friday).

One small mercy for Anne Williams was at the time of her sentence, it had become common practice for the hangman to tie a rope around the prisoner's neck and strangle her before the flames had risen high enough to burn her alive.

Anne Williams was the last woman in Gloucestershire to be burnt at the stake, but another 19 women in England and Wales suffered this punishment after her.

Prison record for Anne Williams

The very last burning of a woman at the stake took place on Wednesday 18 March 1789; Catherine Murphy (also known as Christian Bowman) her crime being 'coining' which came under the High Treason Act. Her execution was carried out at Newgate, London.

These acts and the law did not differentiate between both adult offenders and child offenders. Children as young as 7 and below were hanged alongside adults; below are just two examples,

15-year-old John Smith was hanged at Newgate, London on the 20 of June 1825 for house burglary. His partner, William Mills, age 22, was also condemned but reprieved.

In March 1794, fifteen-year-old Elizabeth Marsh from Dorchester was convicted of the murder of her grandfather, John Nevil. Under the law of the Murder Act of July 1752, she was required to be hanged two days later; this would have been on a Sunday, a day on which executions were not permitted. This being the case she was given an extra day's grace.

Elizabeth would have been kept in chains and allowed only bread and water between her sentence and execution. She was hanged on Monday 17th March and was the first person to be executed outside the new County Gaol in Dorchester. Her body was afterwards given to local surgeons for dissection.

1835 saw the end of capital punishment for crimes other than murder or attempted murder.

DRINK

PC John Joseph Charlton was the village policeman of East Hendred, in Berkshire, from 1887 until he died in 1899.

At the time of his death, he was living with his wife Emily and their four children at Queens Square, East Hundred. There was a fifth child William who was tragically killed in 1894 when a wagon ran over him.

On the evening of Easter Monday 3 April 1899, Isaac Day, landlord of the Chequers public house in Harwell, was being run ragged by his noisy customers most, of whom had been drinking for the best part of the day. Joseph Slatter was singing and passing his hat around begging for money, encouraged by his friend Robert James. For Isaac, this was the last straw, so he asked the two men to leave, but they refused, and Isaac sent for the police.

Shortly, PC Thomas Hewett arrived with PC Charlton to remove the two men, and after a struggle, the two troublemakers were removed from the pub. However, this was not the end of the matter, as once outside, Slatter shouted to Robert James to knife the policemen and he would back him up. A fight broke out between the four men which resulted in both policemen falling to the ground. PC Charlton came off worse; he hit his head on the kerb and became unconscious. PC Hewitt managed to get back on his feet and handcuffed Joseph Slatter, but Robert James ran off.

PC Charlton, still unconscious, was taken to the Harwell police house where a doctor was summoned, but nothing could be done for him, and he died the following day.

Robert James was arrested and joined Slatter at Wantage police station where both men were charged with murder. Appearing before Mr Justice Day on 16 June 1899, they were convicted of manslaughter and sentenced to 20 years hard labour. Both men were released in 1914.

Below is Robert James's charge record

UK, Calendar of Prisoners, 1868-1929

On the following page, you will see the 1891 census showing PC John Joseph Charlton and his family.

Following on from that, you will see the census of 1901 showing Joseph Slatter serving out his sentence at HMP Portsmouth. (Robert James served his sentence in HMP Dartmoor)

Emily Charlton never remarried, which is shown in the census of 1911, where she can be seen living with three of her sons.

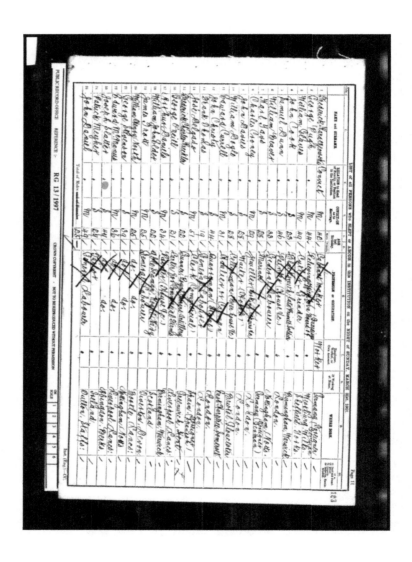

CRIMINAL RECORD OFFICE,
NEW SCOTLAND YARD.

1914.

68

A LIST OF PERSONS coming within the provisions of Sections 5, 7 and 8 of the Prevention of Crimes Act, 1871, discharged, or about to be discharged, from Convict and other Prisons in ENGLAND AND WALES for the week ending 28th March, 1914.

EXPLANATION OF ABBREVIATIONS &c.—p.s., penal servitude; impr., supervision; yrs., years; mos., months; dk., dark; lt., light; ft., feet; gr., grey; tl., hazel; pl., pale; bl., blue; br., brown; bk., black; sr., scar; co., colour; pv., previous conviction; sr., scar; n., right; l., left; tp., tattoo; fn., fair; smy., smartly.

NOTES.—1. The letters preceding the Reg. No. in column No. 2 refer to the years in which prisoner was convicted, e.g., the year 1874 corresponds with the letter "A," 1875 with "B," and so on up to "Z," i.e., 1899. In 1900, the small letter "a" was taken as initial letter of new cycle; thus, for the year 1914 the letter is "o." Prior to 1874, the small letters were used as at present.

2. In the year 1896—which marked the introduction of a scientific method of identification—a system was devised, consequent on which all persons coming within Sections 5, 7, and 8 of the Prevention of Crimes Act were given a yearly number which was retained by them while at large. Upon a subsequent conviction which brought them again within the previously quoted Sections they re-appeared in the Weekly Convict List, and were given a new Office Number. This system involved duplication to a large extent. The Commissioner therefore decided not to give a new Office Number in cases of re-conviction, so it will be noticed that from January, 1903, re-convicted criminals have appeared in the Weekly List under their latest Office Number. The exceptions will be: (a) Those who had received Office Numbers prior to 1896; (b) Discharged prisoners now coming for the first time within the aforesaid Sections.

Office No.	Name (Aliases, Prison, and Register No.)	Date and Place of Birth	Height (without shoes) Ft. In.	Complexion	Hair	Eyes	Marks	Offence (for which), place of Conviction, and Office in Gaol or Place of Committal	Sentence and date of Conviction	Date when Final release or Supervision begins, or Reporting terminates	Date of Liberation, intended Address, and Occupation	Remarks
							LONDON (5th and 8th Section) CASES.				
899-14	Jeremiah O'Brien, alias Jeremiah O'Brien k 356, Dartmoor	1886 London	5 4	fr	bn	bl	prominent ears; sn. cheeks, Wounding— "ERIN-GO-BRAGH," &c., r. "I.L.N.W., J.L.," &c., l. forearm	Wounding— C.C.C. (P.S. Gosling, C.I.D.-B)	5 yrs ps 10-5- 1919	50-5- 1919	27-3-1914 Central Association, London Parker	See 8 17192
898-02	Albert Lee, alias Frederick Perry and Frederick Brooks o h l 520, Portland	1893 Brighton	5 6½	fr	bn	bl	sn. top of forehead and over r. eye; two dots l. forearm	Resolving— Co. of London Sess. (P.S. Bissell, C.I.D.-P)	3 yrs ps 14 related offences 25-3- 1915	25-3- 1915	27-3-1914 Central Association, London Mason	
1459-02	Harry Beach, alias Henry Carter, Henry Green, William Collins, Henry Collins, Henry Weston, George Mitchell, Henry Morris, Jim Riley, Henry Pritchard, William Hardin, Henry Williams, George Green, Harry Long and George Cullen N 8 v o r b 906, Parkhurst	1872 Germany	5 1	fr	bn	bl	sn. l. cheek and l. eyebrow; swelling corner l. eye	Lar—Co. of London Sess. (P.C. Woolett, 200J.)	3 yrs ps 14 related offences 1-3- 1915	27-6- 1914	26-3-1914 London Palmer	Second Licence
1806-08	William Scamp o h 250, Dartmoor	1881 London	5 8	fr	bn	bn	sn. bridge of nose; "J.L.M.B.," forearm, &c., r., bracelet, &c., l. forearm; "J.L.M.B.," r. hand; dot web l. thumb; ring three l. finger	House-stealing— Middlesex Sess. (P.S. Clark, C.I.D.-N)	5 yrs ps & 3 yrs supn. 4-6- 1919	22-6- 1915 (80 days appeal &c.)	27-3-1914 Central Association, London Crutee	
							PROVINCIAL (5th and 8th Section) CASES.				
400-14	John Gilbert g 903, Maidstone	1867 Charlton, Glos.	5 9½	ww	dk bn	gr	sn. l. forehead and across throat; burn on r. wrist; five dots l. forearm	Wounding— Bristol Assizes (Ireland)	10 yrs ps 28-11- 1908	27-11- 1916	27-3-1914 Central Association Labourer	See S 59771 Requirements of Sec. 5 remitted
401-14	Robert James s 131, Dartmoor	1871 Birmingham	5 7	fr	bn (tg gr)	bl	sn. each eyebrow and centre fore-head; several dots r. forearm	Man-slaughter— Reading Assizes (Wantage)	10 yrs ps 14-6- 1909	13-6- 1919	27-3-1914 Central Association Labourer	Requirements of Sec. 5 remitted
402-14	Benjamin Brown f 304, Portland	1861 Woodham Mortimer	5 9	fr	br (tg gr)	bl	long sn. l. thumb	Incest— Chelmsford Assizes (Essex)	4 yrs ps 31-1- 1911	16-3- 1915 (12 days appeal &c.)	26-3-1914 Central Association Blacksmith	Requirements of Sec. 5 remitted

Page's 41-42 shows the discharge papers of Robert James and Joseph Slatter.

The papers give details of their distinguishing marks, their date of discharge and where they were released to.

They also show how Joseph Slatter ended his days in Moulsford asylum. We presume he was declared insane before the end of his sentence, as he was subsequently placed in the care of an asylum upon his release.

On 30 July 1784, brothers Henry and Thomas Dunsdon were executed for murder. They were hanged at Over near Gloucester; their bodies were then hung in chains near Wychwood Forest in Oxfordshire, where their crime had been committed.

There were three Dunsdon brothers: Thomas, Richard and Henry (Tom, Dick and Harry), also known as the notorious 'The Burford Highwaymen', they were part of a gang operating in the area around Burford in Oxfordshire. The brothers began their life of crime by robbing farmers of their livestock and money as they travelled to market. They would then hide the stolen livestock in Wychwood Forest.

However, Richard had disappeared sometime before the murder; possibly dying from blood loss after having his arm hacked off by one of his brothers to escape from capture during a botched robbery at Tangley Hall, Oxfordshire. The owners of Tangley Hall had been tipped off about a planned robbery on their premises. As Richard put his arm through an opening in the door to remove the bolt, those lying in wait for the brothers grabbed hold of his arm and tied it to the bolt so Richard could not remove it. He shouted to his brothers "Cut! Cut!", so one of his brothers drew his sword and severed off his arm at the elbow.

The downfall of Thomas and Henry came about after a drinking session at Capp's Lodge public house, on the edge of Wychwood Forest.

Events unfolded when Henry Dunsdon pulled out his pistol and shot a waiter named William Harding, who later died of his wounds. On the morning of their execution, Henry acknowledged that his life of crime had led to his sorry end, but he stated that his brother was far less to blame, and tried to keep Tom's spirits up to the last.

As they were being prepared for execution, Henry said to his brother, who was lame in one leg, "Come, Tom, you have but one leg; but you have very little time to stand."

Gloucestershire, England, Prison Records, 1728-1914

of one Thomas Crisp.

Isaac Small — Brought in May 15th 1784 Committed by W. Selwell BD Charged with stealing a Silver Watch the property of one John Coter.

Love Griffiths — Brought in May 20th Comm'd by L Haywood Esq' Charged with stealing in the Dwelling house of one Henry Smith, a Red Cloak a Black Silk Hat, a Handkerchief, a petticoat, a pair of Breeches and several other things of wearing Apparell —

John Gardner alias Walkly — Brought in May 25th Comm by T Gryffin Esq' Charged with stealing from the Tentors 6 Yards of Broad Cloth the property of one Charles Ballinger —

John Collett — Brought in May 27th Comm by P Tarcher Esq' Charged upon Oath and his own Confession with stealing a saddle the property of one Thomas Pettat

John Gough and Daniel Whittington — Brought in May 28th Comm by R Scudamore & Br Bayly Esq' Charged with assaulting Elizabeth Cottle and Robert Case on the highway and taking from the said Elizabeth Cottle 2 Shilings & a Black Cloak her property. —

William Hopkins — Brought in May 29th Comm by J Warren LL D to Answer for being the father of a Bastard Child born on the body of one Betty Loxley

Thomas Dunsdon and Henry Dunsdon — Brought in May 31st Comm by T Bush Esq' Charged with shooting at and dangerously wounding one William Harding —

Emily Gardner, aged 18, was the daughter of Peter and Sarah Gardner who run The Early Dawn Public House in Cheltenham.

On 10 December 1871, Emily Gardner, her younger sister Alice, aged 15, and Fredrick Jones, who was courting Emily, were walking Alice home. As they reached the street where Alice lived, they parted ways, with Fredrick promising to see Emily home safe. Less than an hour later he walked into a police station and admitted that he had killed his sweetheart by cutting her throat. Jones also claimed excessive drinking had caused him to do it as he was jealous of a man who was lodging with Emily and her father.

Emily was interred on 15th December in Plot L, Grave number 1002. We are under the assumption that this is a family plot. Four years earlier, the family sadly buried another daughter; Emily's older sister, Matilda, aged 15, who was interred in the same plot on 26 September 1867.

Their father was interred with them on 18 March 1880, aged just 49, but it does not appear their mother was interred with them; however, she, is interred in the same graveyard.

Fredrick Jones, aged just twenty, was tried at Gloucester Assizes by Mr Justice Keating, on 22 December 1871. He was found guilty and condemned to death. A petition was raised seeking a reprieve but was rejected.

Before Jones was hanged, he made a full confession which was printed in its entirety in many newspapers. His hanging took place on 8 January 1872.

This was to be the first hanging to take place within the walls of the prison; all previous hangings having taken place on the roof of the prison, within view of the public. With this being the case, Jones had to climb several steep steps to reach the platform from which he was to be executed by William Calcraft.

THE CHELTENHAM MURDER.

At the Cheltenham Police Court, on Friday, Frederick Jones, the man charged with the murder of his sweetheart, Emily Gardner, at Cheltenham, on Sunday night last, was again brought up. The prisoner had lost the appearance of stolid indifference he had worn at the previous examination and inquest, and appeared to be suffering much both in mind and body. During the earlier part of the examination he sat down with his head bowed upon his hands, but when the razor was produced for indentification he rose with a cry of horror, and had to be held by two constables. From that time there were frequent painful scenes. Whenever the weapon or the body was mentioned or the scene of the murder described, the prisoner wailed piteously, exclaiming one occasion, "Oh God, let me die!" Once he struggled wildly, and cried out, "Oh, my darling Emily;" and when the several wounds were being described, he exclaimed, "What another, and another!" It was not until the depositions had been read that he regained anything like self-possession, but he then heard with composure the announcement of his committal on the charge of murder. He had to be assisted from the dock by two constables.

22 December 1871/ Monmouthshire Merlin

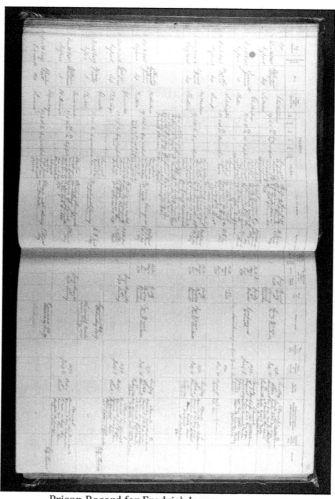

Prison Record for Fredrick Jones

It was Christmas Eve 1880, and the taproom of the New Inn, Bourton-on-the-Water, was already crowded when Thomas Hill and his father, David, walked in at a quarter past nine. The twenty-two-year-old Thomas, a labourer who had been working away in Yorkshire for several years, had decided to return home and spend Christmas with his father and stepmother.

Thomas was born on 1 November 1857 in Little Rissington, to David Hill and his wife Jane Harris. When Thomas was two, his mother Jane passed away; a little while later, his father married Mary Ann Bolton. You can see the family living together in the 1871 census.

It soon became obvious to everybody in the bar that Thomas had begun celebrating before entering the New Inn. After he and his father got their drinks, Thomas stood in front of the fire and began to sing. Thomas now in a jovial mood took the cap of Edward Hughes and started to hit him with it. Although this was done in a light-hearted way, it went on longer than was necessary.

Charles Palmer, aged 27, who had entered the Inn a few minutes after the Hills, told Thomas to stop, and leave Edward alone, which led to the pair exchanging heated words.

Charles Palmer was born in Bourton-on-the-Water to his namesake Charles Palmer and his wife Anna Palmer, in 1855. After his father's death, his mother went on to marry Stephen Betteridge.

James Mustoe, who was working behind the bar at the New Inn, went to fetch some more beer.

Upon his return, he noticed Thomas had stripped off his coat and waistcoat and was challenging anyone to fight him.

This seemed to have aggravated Palmer; Mustoe was worried about the two coming to blows after their earlier exchange of words. Mustoe decided to remove both of the men from the Inn. Firstly, he escorted Palmer from the premises, and then with the help of Police Sergeant William Sims, who had just entered the Inn, escorted Thomas; still shouting that he could take on any man in Bourton. Thomas's father David Hill, followed his son outside, taking the coat and waistcoat with him, and then returned to the taproom. A little later Palmer came back in; he seemed calmer, so was allowed to stay. Thomas Hill also returned to the taproom and asked for another drink, but Mustoe told him he had already had enough, so he left.

At closing time (ten o'clock), everyone was turned out of the Inn into the cold night. Outside, Thomas Hill was waiting for his father and the other men. As they began their walk home, Hill and Palmer had another disagreement. Both accepted their dislike for one another, and agreed to go somewhere quiet- away from the eyes of the law- and settle their differences. As they walked off together, they were soon joined by Palmer's friend, Charles Mosson.

Hill got worried that he was outnumbered, and he said, "Is there two of you?" Mosson replied that this was nothing to do with him. Palmer then said to Hill, "I suppose you want to go to the top of Rissington Hill to have it out, but

I'm not going". He turned towards his home in Bourton: Hill and Mosson walked with him.

Without warning, Hill took his hand out of his pocket and struck Palmer a blow to the neck, shouting "How do you like that?" Palmer staggered backwards and fell to the ground. Mosson tried to lift Palmer but realised that his friend was seriously injured.

The local doctor, Dr Alfred Burt, who lived on the other side of the road, was called upon to treat Palmer, but it was too late as Palmer was already dead, blood seeping out from a wound on his neck.

Sergeant Sims was coming back towards the inn when he was told what had happened. He went off in search of Thomas Hill and found him at the home of his father. Thomas's stepmother Mary asked Hill if he had stabbed Palmer and he confirmed that he had. She then asked him why, to which he replied, "Why, how would anybody help it when he had four or five men around and one excited?"

On the way to the police station, Thomas told Sergeant Sims he had borrowed a knife from his father to cut some cake and had forgotten he had it until he put his hand in his pocket and pulled it out stabbing Palmer in the neck.

On 26th December, a coroner's inquest was held into the death of Charles Palmer. Dr Alfred Burt, who attended to Palmer on the night of his death, carried out the post-mortem. He concluded the wound to the right side of Palmer's neck was the cause of death. Sergeant William Sims told the inquest about finding Thomas at his father's home and the conversation which had taken place between Thomas and his stepmother then himself.

David Hill, Tom's father, was called to give evidence. He related the events of Christmas Eve at the New Inn but said he had not seen his son strike Palmer, as he was walking ahead of them. He also denied the knife was his, and his son hadn't borrowed one from him. Once all the evidence was heard, the inquest jury returned a verdict of wilful murder against Thomas Hill. He was committed to Gloucester Prison to await trial at the next county assizes.

Thomas Hill's trial took place on Thursday 19 February 1881, before Mr Commissioner Wills QC. The witnesses who had been at the New Inn that Christmas Eve gave their evidence, including David Hill. He said that his son had been angry because Palmer had mocked his singing; which he failed to mention at the coroner's inquest.

Thomas Hill's defence counsel, Mr Darling, asked the jury to return a verdict of manslaughter because Thomas's action had been provoked by those in the inn; especially Palmer, who seemed to have taken an instant dislike to him. He continued that his client's anger was out of character, due to his drunken state, rather than if he had been sober. Thomas also felt he was outnumbered when Mosson joined Palmer, and he used a knife to defend himself, not intending to kill anyone.

The jury retired for about twenty minutes, then returned a verdict of not guilty of murder, but guilty of manslaughter. The judge called Thomas' action a "cruel, cowardly and treacherous deed". He sentenced Thomas Hill to the heaviest penalty he could pronounce in this case, which was penal servitude for his natural life.

From the Census of 1891 (page 57), you can see Thomas Hill serving his sentence in Chatham Prison Gillingham Kent.

Illustrated Police News, 8 January 1881. (Image Copyright The British Library Board)

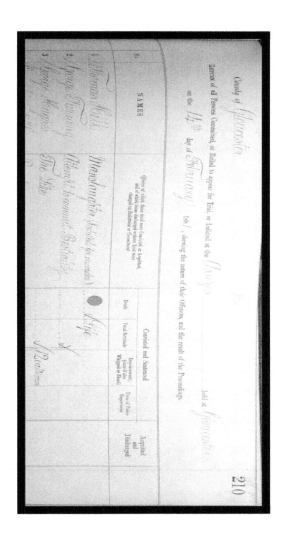

FATAL STABBING CASE IN GLOUCESTERSHIRE.

VERDICT OF WILFUL MURDER.

Mr E. W. Coren, the divisional coroner for Gloucestershire, held an inquest on Tuesday afternoon, at the New Inn, Bourton-on-the-Water, on the body of Charles Palmer (26), who was killed on Christmas Eve, by a stab with a knife. The enquiry was a protracted one, and from the evidence adduced, it appeared that the deceased was in the New Inn on Christmas Eve with several companions, one of whom was named Thomas Hill. The men drank pretty freely, and as the evening advanced Hill become quarrelsome and stripped, challenging a man named Lane to fight. His father interfered, however, but Hill continuing to be quarrelsome he was turned out. At 10 o'clock the house was cleared, when it was found that Hill was waiting outside. He was still quarrelsome, and remarking that he had beaten the best man in Bradford, he said that he would fight any of the ——. On deceased going out some conversation took place between the men, deceased alleging that he knew as much of Yorkshire as Hill. This seemed to irritate the latter, and he challenged deceased to fight, and the men walked on a few yards together, when Hill was observed to pull his hand out of his pocket and to strike the deceased towards his breast, exclaiming as he did so, "How do you like this!" Palmer staggered forward and fell, dying almost instantly, a subsequent examination showing that the two main veins of the neck were severed at their junction. The knife with which the injuries were inflicted was afterwards found at the deceased's home. The jury found a verdict of "Wilful murder," and the accused will be tried at the forthcoming Gloucester Assizes.

1 January 1881 the Cardiff Times

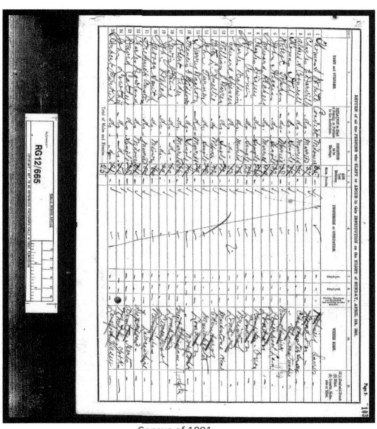

Census of 1891

The Old New Inn, Bourton-on-the-Water, as it is today

View 1

The Old New Inn, Bourton-on-the-Water, as it is today

View 2

The road towards Little Rissington today

Village constable, Walter Creech, was killed whilst on duty in Georgeham, Devon.

Creech was born in 1852 and married in 1881. He and his wife are listed as living in Georgeham, according to the 1881 census. However, we were unable to find out the date when he joined the Devon police force.

Two years later, Walter Creech was stabbed to death by a drunken villager by the name of George Green. On 29 July 1883, outside the King's Arms public house, near the church, Walter had to reprimand Green for the disturbance he was causing. Unfortunately, the man took offence to the caution, whereupon he went to his home and retrieved a knife. He went out once again in search of PC Creech. Upon finding him, Green stabbed the constable in the side, and the wound proved to be fatal.

Green was duly arrested and sent to trial for murder. However, on 8th November, the day of the trial, Green was reported too ill to attend court. He died later that day before he could face the consequences of his actions.

PC Walter Creech left a young widow and a son, who himself did not survive infancy, dying on 7 September 1884.

His grave can be found at

Church of St. George

Chapel Street

Croyde

Georgeham

Brauton

EX33 1QL

Report from the Aberdare Times 10 November 1883

MURDER OF A POLICEMAN.

On Saturday night a Devon county constable, named Walter Creech, was murdered at Georgeham, a village near Barnstaple, by George Green, an old man aged 70. Creech spoke to the prisoner consequent upon his creating a disturbance in a public house, and advised him to go home. Green becoming annoyed went home, and obtaining an old butchering knife returned and stabbed the constable in his side. Creech died early yesterday morning, and Green has been arrested. Deceased, who was thirty years of age, leaves a widow and one child.

A small stream runs through the churchyard.

On the night of 20 September 1877, PC Thomas Bishop was carrying out his round in the village of Bere Regis, when he came across a drunken man by the name of Henry Lock, who had spent the evening drinking in the Drax Arms, a local public house. Being the worse for drink, Lock was singing, shouting and making a nuisance of himself.

Bishop spoke to Lock and asked him to quieten down and go home; warning him that if he did not go home directly, he would escort him personally. However, Lock refused to leave and continued making a noise, so Bishop grabbed hold of Lock's arm and forced him to walk with him to the home of Lock's father.

On reaching the house, Bishop called out for Lock's father to open the door and let his son in. At this point, the two men got into a scuffle and PC Bishop used his baton on him.

As PC Bishop walked away, Lock began shouting at him and picked up a rock and threw it at the policeman.

The rock hit him on the head behind one ear and he fell to the ground. He was stunned, incoherent and bleeding heavily, but was helped to his feet and taken home.

Two hours later, PC Bishop was dead and Henry Lock found himself charged with murder. He was remanded in custody at Dorchester jail to await trial at Winchester Assizes.

At his trial, Lock's defence team stated that PC Bishop had used more force than was necessary in making Lock go home. Lock had several large bruises on his body, which were caused by PC Bishop using his baton on Lock.

This being the case, his defence team asked for the lesser charge of manslaughter to be accepted, which it was, and he was sentenced to 10 years hard labour.

His grave can be found at the address below

St John the Baptist

Southbrook

Bere Regis

Wareham

BH20 7LH

BRUTAL MURDER OF A POLICEMAN.

A brutal murder has been committed at a village near Dorchester. The victim is Police-constable Bishop, 36, who had been 16 years in the Dorsetshire Constabulary. Bishop interfered in a drunken disturbance, and endeavoured to get a man named Henry Lock to go home. There was a scuffle a few yards from Lock's house, and Lock threw a stone which knocked Bishop down. The constable was picked up by some bystanders, but Lock again knocked him down, and while on the ground Bishop was struck by several stones. He has since died. Lock is in custody.

Monmouthshire Merlin 28 September 1877

Page 84

BURIALS in the Parish of *Bere Regis*
in the County of *Dorset* in the Year 18*77*

Name.	Abode.	When buried.	Age.	By whom the Ceremony was performed
Mary Gould No. 665	Ball Lane Bere Regis	May 7th	49	John Fane Langford (Vicar)
Sarah Forthover No. 666	Blackwater Hawley Hants	May 12	75	John Fane Lang (Vicar)
Margaret Lockyer No. 667	Bere Regis	June 19th	75	J.F. Langford (Vicar)
Frederick Smith No. 668	Roke in Bere Regis	July 25th	13 months	W. Osborn B. Allen Curate
John Joiner No. 669	Bere Regis	Sept 5	85	J.F. Langford Vicar
Thomas Bishop No. 670	Bere Regis	Sept 24	89	J.F. Langford (Vicar)
Susan Stroud No. 671	Shitterton in Bere Regis	October 22nd	75	W. Osborn B. Allen Curate
Emily Day No. 672	Bere Regis	Dec 7	33	J.F. Langford Vicar

The grave of PC Thomas Bishop

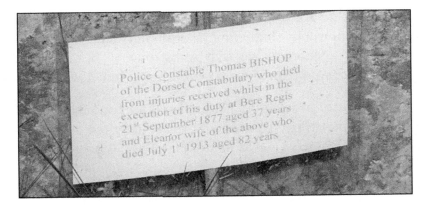

KILLER SERVANTS

Captain William Pierce A'Court of Heytesbury in Wiltshire was planning a trip to Cheltenham, with his wife Katherine, their three daughters and four servants, including footman Joseph Armstrong, who was hired shortly before the excursion to Cheltenham. Katherine took an instant dislike to Armstrong and when valuables began to go missing from the house, she was sure that he was responsible. Katherine shared her fears with her husband and requested that Armstrong be dismissed. It would appear no immediate action was taken.

Shortly after arriving in Cheltenham, Katherine became ill. Her symptoms persisted and increased over ten days, until she died in agony, on 23 September 1776. A post-mortem found she had been poisoned. Captain A'Court immediately suspected that Armstrong was responsible for his wife's death. He had Armstrong's belongings searched, and in his personal chest, they found some of the family's missing valuables, plus two empty arsenic papers.

By this stage, Armstrong had left Cheltenham in a hurry. A pursuit began, but he hadn't travelled far before he was apprehended. Armstrong protested his innocence throughout the trial but the case was proven against him and he was sentenced to death. His body was to be handed to the surgeons for dissection.

On the morning of his execution 17 March 1777, the jailer went to Armstrong's cell to escort him to the gallows, at which point the prisoner requested a few moments to himself to pray.

In those few moments, Armstrong hanged himself with a leather strap, cheating the gallows, but not punishment. His body was hung in chains, as close to the scene of the murder as possible.

Katherine A'Court was buried in St Mary's churchyard Cheltenham where a marble tablet was erected in the church chancel, to her memory.

Joseph Armstrong's Prison Record

Ann Heytrey was a 21 year old from Warwickshire who worked as a servant in the household of Joseph Dormer, a local farmer who lived at Dial House Farm, Ashow, along with his wife Sarah 47, six children and four servants including Ann.

Ann was born in Charlecote Wellesbourne, to William and Mary Heytrey, in 1798. She had a brother Thomas, a blacksmith, who was known to consort with thieves. We will be discussing him in a later chapter.

On Sunday 29 August 1819, Joseph Dormer invited two of his business associates to join him and his family at a village fete. After a morning of enjoying the festivities, Joseph, his guests, and family returned to Dial House for lunch. Around six that evening, Joseph suggested an evening walk to everyone; his children and guests accompanied him. However, Sarah Dormer and Ann Heytrey stayed behind.

At half-past six, Sarah Dormer's niece and nephew paid a visit to Dial House; Sarah gave them each a glass of wine and some cucumbers. Shortly afterwards whilst passing by Dial House, Elizabeth Jaggard saw Sarah in the window, wearing her spectacles, with a book in her hand. She also saw Ann Heytrey leaving the house and gazing up the lane. This was to be the last sighting of Sarah alive.

Ann had returned to the kitchen to where Sarah Dormer was reading and knocked her off her chair.

Sarah recovered quickly and fled upstairs. Ann chased her with a knife she had taken from the pantry, and launched a horrific attack on her after which she left the knife beside the body to give the impression Sarah had 'destroyed herself'.

Around ten minutes past seven, four of the Dormer children arrived home and found Ann acting oddly, and their mother missing. Ann gave two different explanations as to where she was. The eldest daughter, Elizabeth, 17, went upstairs to her room, followed by Mary, 14, who pushed open the door of her mother's room to be greeted by a horrific scene. Her mother lay in a pool of blood. There was only one suspect; Ann Heytrey.

Ann's conduct after her arrest was described as "very proper and correct", with her "acknowledging her guilt for several months before her trial took place". However, she could not explain why she killed her mistress. At first, it was thought her brother Thomas had been involved but Ann denied it. She was asked if she and Sarah had been arguing but again she denied it and swore she would have done anything for her mistress. The only explanation she could give was a 'voice' in her head had told her to kill her mistress. Ann was brought before Sir William D Best at the Warwick Lent assize, on 10 April 1820, and within an hour and a half, she was found guilty and sentenced to hang.

Ann was **executed** on the morning of 12 April 1820, and afterwards, her body was taken down and delivered for dissection.

What makes this case even sadder is before Sarah Dormer's murder; Ann had been caught trying to steal banknotes from the Dormers house. However, the Dormers believed her brother Thomas was behind the incident, and as the family was fond of Ann, Sarah Dormer had urged her husband to drop the charges and insisted that she continued to work for them. Ann had been saved from transportation, or worse still, she could have been hanged.

Sarah Dormer is buried in Assumption of Our Lady Churchyard, Ashow, Warwickshire,

On the next pages, you will see the burial record of Sarah Dormer which shows her age as 57 but her headstone records her age as 47. You will also see Ann Heytrey's prison record.

BURIALS in the Parish of _Ashow_
in the County of _Warwick_   in the Year 1818

Name.	Abode.	When buried.	Age.	By whom the Ceremony was performed.
Hannah Manton No. 17.	Ashow	August 6th	65 and upwards	J. G. Staunton Curate
Ann Lee No. 18.	Ashow	Jany 3. 1819	41 & upwards	J. G. Staunton Curate
Eliz. Shaid No. 19.	Ashow	Jany 10	73 & upwards	J. G. Staunton Curate
Clarke Freeman No. 20.	Ashow	Feby 1	77 & upwards	J. G. Staunton Curate
Elizabeth Kirns No. 21.	Ashow	April 2	7 & upwards	J. G. Staunton Curate
Edward Unwall No. 22.	Ashow	May 29	17 & upwards	J. G. Staunton Curate
William Walter No. 23.	Ashow	July 26	66 & upwards	J. G. Staunton Curate
Sarah Dormer No. 24.	Ashow	Sept. 1	56	J. G. Staunton Curate

England & Wales, Criminal Registers, 1791-1892

On 7 September 1926, the two sisters Eleanor Drinkwater Woodhouse, 65, and Martha Gordon Woodhouse, 57, were shot by their butler, Charles Houghton, 45, at their home Burghill Court, near Hereford.

Charles Houghton was a long time employee of the Woodhouse family. He had initially been taken on as a footman before rising to the position of butler. Charles had been in service for 22 years when he became an alcoholic which began affecting his work. Eventually, on 6 September 1926, Eleanor and Martha Woodhouse had no choice but to dismiss him. Due to his length of service, Charles was offered a month's pay and asked to leave by the following day. However, he protested at being given such short notice, so the sisters told him he had until the end of the week.

The following morning everything appeared to be normal; Charles attended family prayers and served breakfast. However, shortly afterwards tragedy struck, when he shot both sisters. The cook raised the alarm; on arrival at the house, the police had to break into Charles's room, where he had barricaded himself, to discover he had attempted to commit suicide having cut his throat with a razor. He survived; the cut proved to be superficial.

At his trial, Houghton insisted that he had suffered a fit of epilepsy during the shooting. His solicitors tried to plea insanity hoping that it might save Houghton, but to no avail; he was found guilty and given the death sentence.

An appeal was made against the sentence but this was withdrawn. At 8 am on Friday 3 December 1926, Houghton was executed by Thomas Pierrepoint, assisted by Robert Wilson, at Gloucester prison.

The two sisters are buried in the same grave in St Mary the Virgin Burghill churchyard.

On the following page, you can see the census from 1911, showing the residence of Burghill Court, which included the two sisters and Charles Houghton.

We have also included Charles Houghton's prison record.

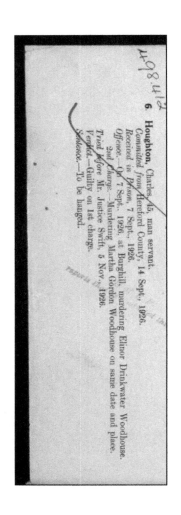

6. **Houghton**, Charles, 45, man servant.
Committed from Hereford County, 14 Sept., 1926.
Received in Prison, 7 Sept., 1926.
Offence.—On 7 Sept., 1926, at Burghill, murdering Elinor Drinkwater Woodhouse.
2nd Charge.—Murdering Martha Gordon Woodhouse on same date and place.
Tried before Mr. Justice Swift, 5 Nov., 1926.
Verdict.—Guilty on 1st charge.
Sentence.—To be hanged.

CENSUS OF ENGLAND AND WALES, 1911.

FILICIDE

In a Dowdeswell field on 15 December 1817, a man saw a woman later identified as Ann Tye (also spelt Tigh) aged 33, in distress. He also saw a small body on the ground next to her and heard a small cry from the body. While he went for help, Ann carried her newborn daughter into nearby woods and forced moss and dirt into the child's mouth. Ann then wrapped her in two aprons and a cloak and proceeded to cover the child's body with moss and dirt.

About an hour later, Ann was found wandering around the woods. When asked where the child was, she denied ever having given birth. Ann was taken home and the search for her child continued until they found the youngster close to death. Sadly all efforts to save her were in vain and she passed away shortly after she was found. (On 15 December the child was christened Phebe Tye).

Ann was arrested and committed to Northleach Gaol. She appeared before the Lent Gloucester Assize on 1 April 1818 and was indicted on four counts. She was found guilty of murder and was sentenced to death. However Ann's execution was temporarily suspended on a point of law, but she was told not to expect a reprieve.

The wording of the indictment was the cause of the temporary reprieve. Was the cause of death suffocation or strangulation?

At the trial, two doctors were called to give evidence. One felt the cause of death was strangulation, while the other believed death was caused by the damage to the throat, when was moss was being forced down it.

The jury had found Ann guilty of causing Phehe's death by the injury to her throat, caused by the moss being forced into it. The Judge felt the indictment did not quite fit the guilty verdict.

Several judges gathered to consider the case and agreed the primary cause of death was suffocation from the moss being forced into the throat. It was felt this did not necessarily need to be included in the original indictment process.

On the morning of 4 May 1818, Ann Tye was executed, after which her body was taken to Northleach for burial.

[Page:]

BURIALS in the Parish of _Northleach_
in the County of _Gloucester_ in the Year 181_

Name.	Abode.	When buried.	Age.	By whom the Ceremony was performed.
Thomas Shepherd No. 70	Northleach	Jan 22 1810	67	Charles Blencowe Curate
George Hall No. 71	Northleach	Jan 26		Charles Blencowe Curate
Elizabeth Mary Holt No. 72	Northleach	Jan 29		Charles Blencowe Curate
Elizabeth Berry No. 73	Northleach	March 15	65	Charles Blencowe Curate
Ann Tye No. 74	Northleach	May 12		Rev. J. Jon... Officiating Minister

Page 2.

BURIALS in the Parish of _Dowdeswell_
in the County of _Gloiter._ in the Year 18_17_

Name.	Abode.	When buried.	Age.	By whom the Ceremony was performed.
Elizabeth Caudle No. 9.	Dowdeswell	January the 20.	18	Rev. W. Baker Rector
Phebe Tigh. No. 10.	Dowdeswell	December the 19. a few hours		Rev. W. Baker Rector

Phehe's Burial record

Phehe's Baptism record

Ann Tye's prison record

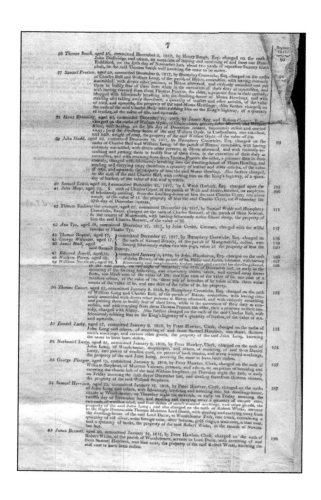

The church of St Peter & St Paul Northleach, where Ann Tye was buried

Little is known about the early life of Anne Greene, except that she was born in 1628, in Steeple Barton, Oxfordshire. At the age of 22, she was employed as a scullery maid, in the household of Sir Thomas Reade, a Justice of the peace, whose residence was at Duns Tew, Oxfordshire. While working in the household she was either seduced or raped by Reade's teenage grandson Geoffrey Reade, reports on his age very between 16 and 17.

From this encounter, she became pregnant, though she later claimed that she was not aware of her pregnancy until she gave birth to a stillborn baby in the privy. Anne was confused and afraid of what to do next, so concealed the body in the corner of the said privy. When the body was discovered, Anne was charged with the infanticide of her baby, by the order of Sir Thomas, who insisted she was charged under the Concealment of Birth of Bastards Act of 1624, which presumed that a woman who concealed the death of her illegitimate child had presumably committed murder.

Testimony from a midwife concluded the baby was premature; the midwife went on to say she 'did not believe that it ever had life.' Despite the testimony of the midwife supporting Anne's claim that the baby was stillborn, Anne was convicted of murder and condemned to death.

On 14 December 1650, Anne was executed at Oxford Castle. At her own request, several of her friends pulled on her swinging body, and a soldier standing by, struck her severely with his musket, to make sure that she was dead.

After half an hour she was cut down and pronounced dead by the prison doctor. Anne was then placed in a coffin and taken to physicians William Petty and Thomas Willis of Oxfordshire University for dissection.

You would think this would be the end of the story, but it's not.

When Petty and Willis opened Anne's coffin, they found she had a faint pulse and was breathing shallowly. Immediately Petty and Willis sought the help of their Oxford colleagues Ralph Bathurst and Henry Clerke. The group of physicians tried many remedies to revive Greene, including pouring hot cordial down her throat, rubbing her limbs and extremities, bloodletting, and applying a poultice to her breasts. They then placed her in a warm bed with another woman, who rubbed her body to help keep her warm. Greene slowly began to recover, and after fourteen hours of treatment she began to speak, and about four days later she started eating solid food. Apart from suffering amnesia about the time surrounding her execution, Anne made a full recovery within a month.

As Anne survived her execution, it was declared an act of God and she was granted a full pardon from the authorities. Following her recovery, Greene went to stay with friends in the country, taking the coffin with her. Subsequently, Anne married and had three more children. She passed away in 1659.

Coincidentally Sir Thomas Reade died three days after Greene's execution; on that note, we end the story of Anne Greene.

On 1 March 1905, James Knight was urgently called home from his place of work at Cossaus and Knights Stationers. His wife of nine years and the mother of his three children, Alice Isbell Knight, had taken a pair of fire tongs and battered their youngest and only daughter, three-year-old Olive Lilian Knight (the spelling of Lilian is how it appears on all records) about the head with them. Olive was rushed to the local hospital but sadly nothing could be done for her.

Alice Isbell Knight was born in Plymouth, Devon, to oil and colour merchant, Frederick Ivey and his first wife, Eliza Clara Neame. Her early life appears quite normal and, up to her marriage in 1896, she lived with her parents and helped in the family shop. Her mother passed away in 1891.

After her marriage to James Knight in 1896, they moved to Cheltenham where, in 1897, she gave birth to the first of three children, Harry Cyril Knight, Edgar James Knight in 1899, and then Olive Lilian Knight in 1902. Money does not appear to have been a problem, as there was a live-in servant.

In the months before the tragedy, it was said Alice Knight had been suffering from depression and, on this particular day, in a moment of insanity, and finding herself alone with her daughter, she picked up the tongs and seriously assaulted her.

The domestic servant, Daisy Radcliffe, entered the room to find Alice Knight holding the bloody tongs and the child severely wounded; Alice uttered the words " I have killed Olive".

Alice was arrested and duly charged with the wilful murder of her daughter and sent to Broadmoor Lunatic Asylum where she spent the rest of her life.

We didn't want to end the story there so we researched into what happened to James Knight and his two sons after the tragedy.

We then discovered from the 1911 census that James Knight and his two surviving children moved to Burnham-on-Sea, where James opened a shop selling books and stationery. It would appear that James kept the shop until around 1914. After that, we lost track of James and his children, and after a long search, we could not find a trace of James or his sons in any English records.

We then discovered one Harry Cyril Knight serving in the Australian Army during World War One. 'Could this be James and Alice Knight's son?' we thought.

It was then we also discovered that Harry was not the only one to serve with the Australian Army during World War One. His father James and his brother Edgar both joined up with Harry on the same day, the 8th of January 1916. Their service numbers: 1668, 1669, 1670 and all served with the 49th Infantry and all three survived the war, returning to Australia in 1919. All three men list Alice Isbell Knight as their next of kin, her address being at Broadmoor.

We could find no record of them leaving England, but do know from their service records that they made a home for themselves in Bundaberg, Queensland.

James Knight passed away on 25 May 1946, Harry Cyril Knight passed away on 4 April 1972, followed shortly after by his brother Edgar James Knight on 23 June 1972. All three are buried in Queensland.

Alice Knight passed away in 1949, aged 82.

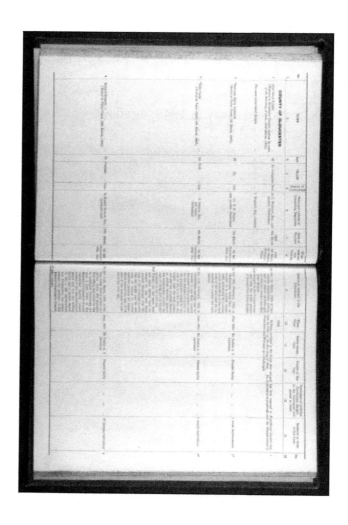

Alice Isbell Knight's prison record

On Saturday 13 November 1897, Stratford police arrived at Drybank Farm, Ettington, and began digging up the farmhouse garden. They had in their custody, Elizabeth Brandish, a 33-year-old unmarried nurse, who was suspected of having murdered her illegitimate son, Rees Thomas Yelves Brandish, aged just two-and-a-half. After digging around the farmhouse garden for a while, they found the body of a little boy buried beneath the cabbages, doubled up, and covered in quicklime.

Elizabeth Brandish, 33, was born in Moreton-in-Marsh, in 1858, to Samuel Brandish and his wife Elizabeth. In 1895 Elizabeth gave birth to an illegitimate boy in Dover; she claimed Reese's father was a man who had seduced her on a train three years earlier. When she told him of her pregnancy, he denied everything. Elizabeth couldn't look after her son as she needed to earn a living, but work could be lost if potential employers found out she had a child out of wedlock. Elizabeth using the name 'Mrs Edwards' paid Thomas and Susannah Post five shillings a week to look after her son. They lived with their niece Sarah Urben, at Wye, near Ashford in Kent. While she found work in Clent, north Worcestershire, this arrangement went on from when Rees was nine weeks old until just after his second birthday.

On 9 September 1897, Elizabeth Brandish arrived at the Post's house and told them she was taking Rees to the farm her brother George worked at in Ettington (It later turned out he had no idea that his sister had been pregnant, and given birth to a son).

Despite the Posts' protest, she took Rees, but none of his clothes; however, she did promise to write with news about him.

On 11th September, Elizabeth arrived at Ettington looking distressed. She had a tin box, but there was no sign of her son. In the meantime, the Post's had contacted the vicar at Ettington airing their concerns for Rees, but he had not seen the child. Suspicions aroused, the police began making enquiries and on the 22nd October arrived at the house where Elizabeth was staying at Clent, Worcestershire. They took her into a private room where she was asked if she had a son and if so where was he. She first refused to answer and told them it was none of their business; however, she then confessed that she did have a son and she'd given him away to a stranger on a train. A search began for the mystery woman based on the description Elizabeth had provided. The police arrested Elizabeth on 9th November. On 13th November police gave up searching for the mystery woman and decided to dig up the Drybank Farm garden. They discovered the body of a child.

On 15th November an inquest into the child's death took place at, The Chequers Inn, Ettington. It ended with a verdict of wilful murder against Elizabeth Brandish.

The first trial of Elizabeth Brandish for the wilful murder of her son started on 10 March 1898 at the Warwick Assize. Elizabeth entered a plea of not guilty and insisted she had given Rees away to a stranger. After three days of debating, the jury was unable to reach a verdict, and so was discharged. A second trial was ordered which began at the Summer Assizes, on 28th July, before Mr Justice Darling.

A motive was offered by the prosecution that Elizabeth wanted to hide the evidence of her illegitimate son Rees because she wanted to marry a policeman, Sgt Robert Nerromore, who knew nothing of her past.

Witnesses were called and reported seeing Elizabeth and her child at various times during their train journey on 11th September. Elizabeth and her son were seen travelling in a third-class train compartment bound for Bletchley, changing at Blisworth for a second train for Banbury, and then getting off at Towcester at 4.50 pm, where Elizabeth paid the excess for a second-class carriage. However, by the time she got off the train at Ettington, at 8 pm, Elizabeth was alone. The porter at Ettington stated that Elizabeth alighted with a 'light' box, and carrying a bundle. The carrier who transported her to Dry Bank Farm, on the other hand, reported that the box was 'heavy', and Elizabeth had no bundle.

Most of the evidence was circumstantial and the trial ended with an unexpected result. After an hour and a half of deliberation, the jury returned with a not guilty verdict. Justice Darling seemingly disgusted with the verdict left the court without telling Elizabeth she was free to go.

The body was never fully identified as being that of Rees because the quicklime had destroyed the face. What was known for sure was that the body was that of a 2-and-a half-year-old male, and death was considered to be suffocation. Poor Rees was given a pauper's burial, in the Holy Trinity churchyard in Ettington paid for by the parish, and the only people present for the burial were the undertaker and his wife.

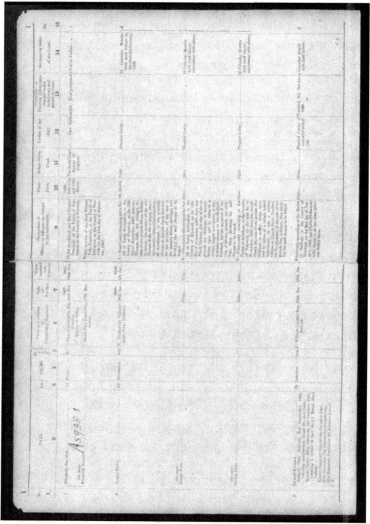

On the next two pages are the records from her trial.

NURSE BRANDISH.

The charge against Nurse Brandish was, it will be remembered, that of murdering her little child. At Ettington, near Stratford-on-Avon, Mr. Christopher, coroner for South Warwickshire, resumed the inquiry into the circumstances connected with the death of a boy, aged two and a half years, alleged to be the illegiti-

mate son of Elizabeth Brandish, a nurse, who is in custody upon a charge of wilful murder. The body was found buried in a garden at Drybank Farm, Ettington. A large number of witnesses were examined and a good deal of correspondence between the prisoner and the child's foster parents was read. The jury after half an hour's deliberation, returned a verdict of wilful murder against Elizabeth Brandish, the mother.

Holy Trinity churchyard Ettington, where Rees lays in a pauper's grave, with no headstone.

His uncle George Brandish is also buried here, his grave

marked, now with a broken headstone.

Rees cousin Fredrick who was killed was killed in WW1 is also remembered on the stone.

MURDER AND SUICIDE

The following story has been constructed using newspaper reports and records and may not be 100 % correct. Elizabeth Humphries, aged 46, was born in Cheltenham, according to the census of 1901, but some newspaper articles from the time say she was from Wales. In the same census, she is listed as single, but again some papers stated she was a widow. As you can see, Elizabeth Humphries is a bit of a mystery.

Sometime after 1891, she moved into the home of Joseph Harper as a lodger. During this period she also gave birth to a daughter. The name of the father is not revealed in any source and there is no indication that Joseph Harper was the father. In March 1901, the relationship between the Harpers and Elizabeth, for whatever reason, seems to have soured, and Elizabeth was given notice to leave. After leaving the Harpers, Elizabeth then began to encounter problems with Joseph Harper. He would follow her around and constantly harass her to the point that Elizabeth had to keep changing lodgings. Warnings from the police, and even being bound over to keep the peace after he had assaulted Elizabeth, did not deter Harper from making her life miserable.

Events finally came to a head in September 1901, when Elizabeth Humphries was walking home from her job. She was approached by Joseph, who attacked her, cutting her throat. He then turned the knife on himself, therefore killing them both.

Elizabeth and Joseph are buried in the same cemetery, but Joseph Harper was buried without a service.

CHELTENHAM TRAGEDY.

Victim's Brother a M chen Man.

A double inquest on the victims of the Cheltenham tragedy was held by Mr. Waghorne on Tuesday afternoon. From the evidence it appeared that Miss Elizabeth Humphries, who had lived in Cheltenham for many years, but whose brother resides at Machen, near Newport, lived for about nine years as a lodger with a married couple named Harper. During her residence with them Miss Humphries was confined of a child, in which Harper always took an interest, though its paternity was never made known. Some six months or so ago differences arose, and Miss Humphries received notice to leave, which she obeyed. Harper for assaulting her was bound over by the magistrates in July last. Since that time he has persistently followed the woman about and so threatened her that she had to seek police protection. When returning home from work on Saturday afternoon Harper, who was about 60 years of age, jostled against her in the street, and spoke to her, but she went on her way without taking any notice. She had not proceeded far, however, before Harper darted back, and in the middle of a street crossing, in full view of the windows of a crowded public-house, seized her by the hair, pulled her head back, and with a razor nearly severed it from the body. Harper turned the razor upon himself and ended his own life.— The Jury found that Miss Humphries was wilfully murdered by Harper, against whom a verdict of felo de se was returned.

A GHASTLY TRAGEDY.

MURDER AND SUICIDE AT CHELTENHAM.

The fashionable town of Cheltenham was aroused to a high pitch of excitement on its becoming known that a murder had been committed in one of the public streets. The victim was Elizabeth Humphries, a widow, who with a child eight years of age had formerly lodged with Joseph Harper, by whose hand she met her death. In July last she summoned him for assault, and he was bound over to keep the peace. This seems to have greatly incensed him, and it is pretty clear that he harboured a grudge against the woman, who left his house by his notice and took lodgings elsewhere. He appears to have kept in touch with her whereabouts, and only a week ago she again changed her lodgings. He ascertained where she had gone, and inquired at the adjoining house for her. From a statement by the child it is believed that he intended mischief, but by what means was not known, although poison was spoken of.

About six o'clock on Saturday evening Harper was with his wife in Albion Street, which is much frequented, when he saw Mrs. Humphries, and said to his wife "There she is." He attacked Mrs. Humphries with a razor, and before anyone had time to stop him he inflicted a great gash across her throat, which severed the carotid artery and windpipe. She immediately died. The assailant then cut his own throat. A doctor was quickly on the spot, and after rendering temporary aid sent the man to the hospital, where he expired soon after arriving there. Harper was a labourer, and his victim, who was a charwoman, was regarded as a quiet, respectable, hard-working woman.

9 November 1901 Rhyl Record and Advertiser

CHELTENHAM TRAGEDY.

Funeral of a Murderer and His Victim.

The funeral of Miss Elizabeth Humphries, of Cheltenham, who was murdered on a street crossing on Saturday last by her former landlord, Joseph Harper (who afterwards took his own life, and against whom a coroner's jury returned a verdict of felo de se), took place on Friday afternoon at Cheltenham Cemetery, when the mourners included Mr. and Mrs. John Humphries of Machen, near Newport, and Mr. Joseph Humphries and Miss Humphries, of Bristol. When the mourners had departed there were several pathetic scenes among the many people who thronged to the graveside, and who had known Miss Humphries for many years. On the previous day Harper was buried in a secluded spot in the same cemetery, but without any burial service. In its passage through the streets the procession was several times greeted with groans and execrations.

6 November 1901 Evening Express

Overview Cheltenham Cemetery

Before living in Cheltenham, both Lily Lyons and John Lyons resided in Birmingham (1901 census).

Both Lily and John were born in Birmingham; John was born in 1876, and Lily 10 May 1879. They married in 1896 and four of their five children were born here also. The fifth child, Arthur Edward Lyons, was born in Cheltenham in 1903. Together with their five children, the Lyons family lived on the business premises of the Electro Plating Company for which John worked.

On the afternoon of May 31 1905, Lily Lyons was seen calling for help from her bedroom window. Workers from the company rushed into the house and were met with a terrible sight. John Lyons was lying dead with his throat cut and Lily was seriously wounded with a gash to her throat. She was rushed to the hospital. In the days leading up to the incident, John Lyons had reported that he felt unwell and was unable to work. He also had been arguing with his wife. Amazingly, Lily Lyons survived her injury.

We were intrigued by this story as Lily survived the attack by her husband, and we found out a little more about her life.

We discovered that Lily and her five children moved back to Birmingham. We know this from the 1911 census. In the same year, she also remarried. She must have been a very remarkable woman to have trusted another man. Lily went on to have two more children and lived to the grand old age of 91.

Evening Express 1st of June

A TRAGEDY AT CHELTENHAM.

A shocking domestic tragedy took place on Wednesday afternoon in Fairview-street, Cheltenham, on premises occupied by the Electro-plating Company. One of their workmen, named John Lyons, and his wife and five children resided on the premises, and about four o'clock Mrs. Lyons appeared at the bedroom window calling for help. The manager of the company and neighbours rushed upstairs, and found Lyons lying dead, with his throat terribly gashed. His wife was also shockingly injured in the throat, and lies in hospital in a dangerous condition. All the children were at school, with the exception of a baby, which was found in a room where the tragedy happened, covered with blood, but uninjured. Deceased was a polisher by trade, and is described as a steady man, but it is alleged that there had been frequent rows between him and his wife. He had complained of being unwell for several days, and had not been in business much since Saturday. Lyons was about 28 years of age, and formerly resided in Birmingham.

MISCELLANEOUS

On 16 August 1660, a 70-year-old gentleman named William Harrison, who served the Campden family as a steward, left his home in Chipping Campden, to walk to the village of Charingworth to collect rents. When he did not return that evening his wife sent out a servant, John Perry, to search for him. However, he too failed to return. The next morning, William's son, Edward, set out to find both men. He discovered John on the road to Charingworth and together they continued the search for William.

They found no trace of him and returned to Chipping Campden. News then emerged that some items had been discovered on the main road between Chipping Campden and Ebrington. These included a shredded hat and a blooded neckband identified as belonging to William but there was no sign of the steward, William Harrison.

The local Justice of the Peace, Sir Thomas Overbury, was called upon to open an investigation into Williams' disappearance; his only suspect being John Perry, who was promptly arrested and asked to account for his movements when he had gone in search of his master. He stated that after a fruitless search, but night drew in, and as he was afraid of the dark, had spent about an hour sheltering in a hen-house.

However, around midnight, the moon came out providing enough light for him to resume the search.

He had then lost his way in the mist and had ended up sleeping by the roadside. In the morning, he had begun to make his way back home, at which point he met with Edward Harrison.

After a week in custody, Perry suddenly confessed to Sir Thomas Overbury, that he, his mother Joan and his brother Richard Perry had murdered William Harrison, for the rent money he had collected that day. He continued his story by saying William had been strangled, which appeared odd, as there was blood on the neckband and the items had been hacked and the corpse dumped in a local cesspool.

His mother and brother were promptly arrested and charged with robbery and murder. Both protested their innocence. The local cesspool was dredged and the surrounding area searched but still, nothing was found.

Their first trial took place in September 1660 and dealt with the charge of robbery; as at this point in time, the judge was unwilling to prosecute the three for the murder, without a body being found. Initially, the three accused pleaded not guilty. Their defence counsel however persuaded them, as first-time offenders, they were guaranteed a free pardon under the Indemnity and Oblivion Act of 1660, so they changed their pleas to guilty. This would prove to be a fatal mistake for the accused. All three were granted a pardon under the new act. However, all three remained in jail on the murder charge.

In jail, John continued to blame his mother and brother. He also refused to eat or drink anything, saying they were trying to poison him.

In spring 1661, the court reassembled to deal with the charge of murder. Because William had been missing for nearly a year they believed him now to be now dead.

Unfortunately because of the three's earlier guilty plea to the charge of robbery, they were now deemed to have committed the murder,

This time John Perry joined his mother and brother in pleading not guilty to the murder of William Harrison. John claimed that his original testimony had been false because of insanity. Nevertheless, the jury found all three of the Perrys guilty and they were sentenced to death.

All three were executed on Broadway Hill. The first to be hung was Joan Perry who was believed to have been a witch and had persuaded her sons to commit the crime; the second was Richard and lastly John.

This is where the story gets odd

Two years later (1662), William Harrison returned to Chipping Campden. He gave an extraordinary account including robbery, kidnapping and slavery. William stated that while he was returning from rent-collecting, two men on horseback attacked him with swords and kidnapped him. He was then transported out of England on a ship bound for Turkey, where he was sold as a slave to a physician in Smyrna.

After about a year later, his master died, leaving William to fend for himself. He made his way to a nearby port, where he used a silver bowl from his ex-master's house to buy passage on a ship bound for Portugal. After arriving in

Lisbon, he encountered a fellow Englishman. This man took pity on William, gave him money, and arranged his passage on a ship bound for England.

As the saying goes 'truth is stranger than fiction'.

We discussed this rather strange case and we both find it very hard to believe that anyone would want to kidnap a man of Harrison's age and sell him into slavery. Not to be disrespectful to people of his age, but we are convinced, as a 70-year-old, he would not command much of a price at a slave auction and to be honest, we couldn't think of anybody who would buy a slave of 70 years of age. This begs the question where was William Harrison during these two years?

Another mystery was why did John Perry confess to murder and implicate his mother and brother as his accomplices. Maybe he really was insane or maybe there was a family row and John took his revenge a little too far.

Truth brought to Light. OR,

Wonderful strange and true news from *Gloucester* shire, concerning one Mr. *William Harrison*, formerly
Stewart to the Lady *Nowel* of *Camden*, who was supposed to be Murthered by the Widow *Pery* and
two of her Sons, one of which was Servant to the said Gentleman. Therefore they were all three
apprehended and sent to *Gloucester* Goal, and about two years since arraigned, found guilty, condemned, and Executed upon *Broadway* hill in sight of *Camden*, the mother and one Son being then buried
under the Gibbet, but he that was Mr. *Harrisons* Servant, hanged in Chains in the same place, where
that which is remaining of him may be seen to this day, but at the time of their Execution, they said Mr.
Harrison was not dead, but ere seven years were over should be heard of again, yet would not confess
where he was, but now it appears the Widow *Pery* was a witch, and after her Sons had rob'd him, and
cast him into a Stone Pit, she by her witch-craft conveyed him upon a Rock in the Sea near *Turkey*,
where he remained four days and nights, till a *Turkish* Ship coming by, took him and sold him into *Turkey*,
where he remained for a season, but is now through the good providence of God return'd again safe to
England, to the great wonder and admiration of all that know the same. This is undeniably true, as is
sufficiently testified by the Inhabitants of *Camden*, and many others thereabouts.

To the Tune of, *Aim not too high.*

Today a tower stands on Broadway hill where Joan, Richard and John Perry were executed.

The remains of "Campen House" which was converted into living accommodation for estate servants one of whom was William Harrison who lived here at the time of his disappearance.

A second view of what remains of Campden house

We discovered an unusual tale while looking through the Gloucestershire Prison Records on Ancestry.

On 31 August 1802, Jonathan Thorndell was serving six months in Northleach House of Correction for milking a cow (stealing milk from a cow).

Joining him there were three ladies serving time for stealing wood.

Another gentleman was serving time for leaving his wife and family.

See the next page for the record and also on the next three pages we have included photos of old Northleach prison.

Northleach House of Correction is open to the public

Alice Sarah Theresa Holland was the wife of Colonel Holland of the 2nd Gloucestershire Rifle Volunteers. She was arrested on a charge of larceny in February 1904, and held in a cell at Cheltenham police station. Unfortunately, she had concealed a bottle of oxalid acid on her person, which she used to commit suicide.

It was reported that she had recently taken to drink in recent times and had often spoken of taking her own life.

At the time of writing, we could find no other information about Alice Holland or her husband who appears to have used two different Christian names.

SUICIDE IN A POLICE CELL.

An inquest was held at Cheltenham on Friday on the body of Alice Holland, wife of Mr. Mancklin Holland, for some years colonel of the 2nd Gloucestershire Rifle Volunteers. Deceased was under arrest at Cheltenham on a charge of larceny, and whilst in the cell at the police-station took oxalic acid, which she had secreted about her person. Deceased had frequently given way to drink, and threatened to commit suicide.—A verdict of "Suicide during temporary insanity" was returned.

Weekly Mail 27th February 1904

A spot of grave robbery in the quiet village of Naunton.

RESURRECTIONISTS.—We apprehend there is some foundation for the remark, that the new Police in the Metropolis is so efficient that many of the London thieves and vagabonds are driven to pursue their unhallowed avocations in the country. A few days since the body of a woman, named *Wicksey*, which had been buried on Sunday week in Naunton churchyard, was found under a hayrick near Naunton Inn, on the Stow-road. The spoilers of the sepulchre were disappointed of their booty, which they doubtless intended to convey to London during the night, by the parish officers having ordered the corpse to be re-interred immediately.

Morning Post 24 Dec 1829

One of the many board sheets that can be found, but sadly, are very hard to read.

Next is the unfortunate case of Thomas Roberts, of Buckland, Worcestershire, who was fatally stabbed on 6 April 1750. Thomas received a single stab wound to the body; where is not known, but we do know it was delivered by the hand of one Richard Cull, who was the same age as Thomas. Cull was duly arrested charged with murder.

In July 1750, Richard's mother, Mary Cull, was arrested and charged on suspicion of being accessory to murder. From the records, we also learned that Richard Cull was found guilty on the lesser charge of manslaughter, and burnt on the hand in August 1750. His mother was also convicted and we believe from the record she was also burnt on the hand, but no name is mentioned.

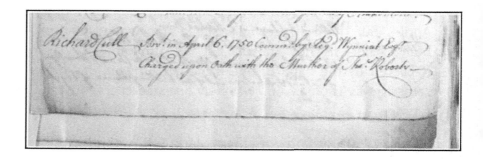

Prison record for Richard Cull

Jul 31. Gloucester, Jul 28. Assizes. RICHARD CULL, for the Murder of THOMAS ROBERTS, and MARY CULL, charg'd on Suspicion of being accessary to that Murder.

Aug 7. Gloucester, Aug 4. Two were burnt in the Hand, viz. RICHARD CULL, for Manslaughter ....

The final verdict

UNSOLVED

On the evening of Saturday 7 May 1780, John Player of Berrow, Worcestershire, was awoken on hearing what he thought, was screaming and thuds coming from the direction of one of his neighbour's home. Disturbed by the sounds, he decided to go round to the house. As he approached, he could hear screaming sounds, but when he knocked on the door, there was no answer and the noise stopped. He went to the back door, where he could hear voices coming from the kitchen and he called out, but again got no reply. He went back home to wake his wife.

They both returned to the house to find the door open, and the house now in silence. Looking through the open door, they saw blood dripping from the kitchen ceiling down onto the floor. With trepidation, Player made his way upstairs where he was shocked to come across what he thought were two bodies. Appalled by the scene before him, he returned downstairs. He and his wife left the property to raise the alarm with the neighbours.

Another neighbour searched more of the upstairs rooms and found not two, but four bodies; these were of Edward Gummery, the head of the household, his wife Elizabeth, and their 9-year-old daughter Anne who were all found in the main bedroom. In the other bedroom was the body of Elizabeth Gummery's brother, Thomas Sheen, who happened to be staying the night. All four had been brutally murdered with a hatchet.

Robbery was ruled out as a motive, as 29/8d in cash was found in the house and 3/6¼d was found on Sheen.

The villagers arrested some local tramps who seemed suspicious, but they were released soon afterwards. Although some blood was found on their clothes, it was deemed insufficient to convict them. No one was ever brought to justice and charged with the crime.

The family are buried in the church of St Faith, Berrow, Worcestershire.

A memorial stone to the Gummery family can be seen on the outside wall of the church.

St Faith, Berrow, Worcestershire

St Faith, Berrow, Worcestershire

An Account of four People cruelly

MURDERED

In their Beds in the Parifh of Berrow near Caftle Moreton in Worcefterfhire, about Six Miles beyond Newent.

ON Sunday Morning laft about 4 o'Clock, a perfon who lived at a fmall diftance from the Houfe where the Murder was committed heard as he thought a groaning, accordingly he went to the Houfe of one Edward Gommery a labouring Man, finding the outward Door faft, he called to them, but receiving no Anfwer he returned Home, and told his Wife that he feared all was not right at Gommery's, as they did not anfwer when he called, he then defired his Wife to go with him to the Houfe : He now found the outward Door open, for the Villains were juft gone away, for they were in the Houfe when he firft came there, having got in at the back part of the Houfe, had the fore Door been open and he had gone in, he would have fallen a Sacrifice to their Fury : But his coming difturbed them, and they left the Houfe.

When they came into the lower Room they called, but receiving no anfwer they went up Stairs, but fhocking was the Scene, for Edward Gommery was lying with one Arm almoft fever'd from his Body, and his Bowels hanging out : His Wife, with the upper part of her Head chopp'd in pieces, and her Nofe cut off : Her Daughter with her Throat cut, and a Wound on the back of her Head : Mrs. Gommery's Brother lay with his Head fplit open, and the Blood ran in Streams through the crevices of the Floor. The Alarm being given, a general fearch began, and three Men with fome Women and Children were found in a field about a quarter of a Mile off. On one of them was found a bloody Stick, and fome Blood was found on the Cloaths of another . They were immediately fecured, and taken to the Place where the Bodies lay, In returning, fays one of them "The Girl looks juft the fame as fhe did when fhe was afleep."

One of them is named Evans, and is a Bafket-maker. Another of them ufed to fell Toafting Forks about the Country.

May 9th, 1780.

In 1944, Florence Porter, 33, otherwise known as Florrie, lived at Little Heath Lane in Lickey End, Bromsgrove, Worcestershire, with her mother. She worked at the Austin Motor Company at Longbridge as a wages clerk. Before the war, she spent her spare time enjoying music and dancing, but on the outbreak of war, she dedicated her spare time to helping the war effort, including joining the St John Nursing Division at Austin Motors.

Around 8 am on Friday 27 October 1944, Florrie's body was found by two boys; ten-year-old Albert Egan, and his friend, seven-year-old Louis Price. They were cycling to school when Albert noticed a blue object (underwear as it turned out to be) under the veranda at the rear of Lickey End School. On closer inspection, he discovered a woman lying on her back. Albert sent Louis to fetch the school caretaker Mrs Perry. She confirmed the boy's story and went to the home of a Mrs Smith; one of the few locals to own a telephone in the area. From there she called the police.

When the body was examined it was found she had been stabbed in the neck and chest. One of the wounds had penetrated her heart, her skirt had been pulled up around her waist, but her underwear was still in place and there were no signs that she had been sexually assaulted. She had also been punched in the face by someone wearing a ring, and blood was found beneath her fingernails.

When the police spoke to her sister Doris, she told them on the evening of Florrie's death, they had walked into Bromsgrove together. Doris explained Florrie had told her she was meeting a man called Hal. They then parted ways.

A witness came forward and told the police she worked as a barmaid at The George Hotel.

On the evening of 26 October 1944, between 9 pm and 9.30 pm, she went into the smoking-room of The George and saw an American officer with a woman. They appeared to be friendly and were laughing and talking. She identified the woman as being Florrie Porter.

The next sighting of Florrie was by a neighbour of the Porters. He was standing on the corner of School Lane at approximately 10.20 pm when, by the light of the lamp on the opposite side of the road, he noticed Florrie walking by with an American officer. This was the last known sighting of Florrie.

At 10-30pm screams were heard by those living close to the School. But as it was a wet and windy night, no one took any notice. Her mother didn't report her missing nor was she worried, because Florrie often stopped overnight at a friend's house in Bromsgrove to save the long walk home.

Bromsgrove Police, Worcester CID and the American military police all worked together to find the murderer. Statements were taken, interviews were held with American officers, and an identity parade took place at the local US army base.

The police even issued an appeal, asking for the officer who was with Florrie Porter that evening to come forward. The American officer and murderer's identity remain a mystery to this day.

Woman Found
Stabbed

THE body of a young woman, who had apparently died from stab wounds in the chest, was found this morning at the rear of Lickey End Council School, near Bromsgrove, Worcestershire.

She was Florence Porter, aged 33, who was employed at the Austin motor works as a time-office clerk and who lived with her widowed mother at Lickey End.

About 10.30 last night she was seen walking towards her home with an American soldier.

Throat, Heart, Lung Stabs

Worcestershire police are seeking a U.S. officer in their inquiries into the death of the 33-years-old V.A.D. nurse, Florence Porter, whose stabbed body was found in a school playground at Lickey End, near Bromsgrove, Worcestershire.

The inquest was opened today and adjourned until December 4. Evidence was given of stab wounds in the throat, heart, and lungs.

High American officers from the Provost Marshal's Department were present and took notes.

Stabbed Woman, Soldier Sought

Inquiries continued to-day into the murder of Florence Porter, 33, a clerk in the Austin motor works, Birmingham, who was found stabbed near her home at Heath-lane, Lickey End yesterday.

Worcestershire Police, with whom the American Military Police are co-operating, are searching for an officer or soldier with blood stained clothes.

A schoolboy found the body under a school verandah.

Several American officers were questioned by the police last night.

On the evening of April 24 1954, unmarried midwife Olive May Bennett, 45, was seen drinking alone in the Red Horse Hotel in Bridge Road. At closing time she was seen waiting outside the hotel for someone who has never been identified. This was the last known sighting of her alive.

The following morning, her body was found wedged against an obstruction on the river bank. It was discovered she had been strangled with a woollen scarf and her body weighed down by a 56lb Victorian gravestone from the church. The body was quickly identified. At the time of her death, she had undergone a bit of a personality change. Previously she led a sheltered existence. Up until her 40s, she led a quiet life, but on reaching her 40s she began dating, drinking, smoking and taking more care with her appearance.

Despite the best effects of the police, which included a thorough search of the area and interviewing all her known associates including the men she had dated, the case, unfortunately, remains unsolved to this day

WEDNESDAY, APRIL 28, 1954

Tombstone Found in River at Stratford Near Woman's Body

New Clues to Mystery of Midwife's Death

Stratford police yesterday dragged from the bed of the River Avon a footstone from a grave in Holy Trinity Churchyard whose headstone bore the inscription: " In the midst of life we are in death."

It may have been used to weight the body of Miss Olive May Gardiner Bennett (45), a midwife, whose body was found in the river about 50 yards further downstream, below the churchyard wall, on Saturday. Police are considering the possibility that she may have been pushed into the river from the top of the wall, with the stone tied to her, after she had been assaulted.

Lying beside the tombstone in the river were the brown felt hat Miss Bennett was wearing when she was last seen alive at 6 p.m. on Friday, her purse containing money, and her black handbag.

Churchyard Searched

Supt. John Capstick, of Scotland Yard, who was in charge of the enquiry into the Carmarthenshire farm murder, went to Stratford yesterday, accompanied by Det.-sgt. Heddon, to help in the investigations.

Visitors to Shakespeare's tomb in Holy Trinity Church were forbidden to enter a large portion of the churchyard while detectives searched the grass and daisies on the tombs near the place from which Miss Bennett may have plunged into the river.

For the first time for many years the Avon was lowered by means of the weirs to help the police in their two-hour drag for the tombstone.

Death on Friday Night

Miss Olive May Bennett

after a post-mortem examination had been made on Monday. " The results

Report from the Birmingham Post 1954 (Thank you to Amanda Harvey Purse for finding the report)

Death on Friday Night

Miss Bennett's body was found on Saturday after the gardener of Holy Trinity, Mr. T. Anderson, of Sanctus Road, had found a pair of spectacles, a shoe and the lower half of a set of dentures on the low wall which guards the churchyard path from the 15ft. drop into the Avon.

Miss Bennett was last seen alive at 8 p.m. on Friday, when she left the Monroe Devis Maternity Home at Tiddington, where she worked, it was stated last night by Det. Chief Supt. Spooner, head of the Warwickshire C.I.D., who accompanied Supt. Capstick throughout his enquiries yesterday.

They spent much of their time at the maternity home questioning the staff and searching Miss Bennett's room and belongings.

The time of death has now been fixed as Friday night, it was stated by Supt. Spooner, who appealed to the public for anyone who saw Miss Bennett that evening or who was near the churchyard to tell the police.

'Known to Frequent Bars'

Miss Bennett, a woman of medium height, with curly, sandy hair, going grey, was wearing a black and grey striped coat and a brown felt hat over a blue woollen dress. She had brown shoes—one of which is still missing—fawn pigskin gloves and a black leather box-type handbag. She wore spectacles with light pink half-frames. She was known to frequent bars in Stratford, Supt. Spooner said.

Miss Bennett announced her intention of going into Stratford when she left the maternity home on Friday evening. It is understood that she intended to meet a friend. She had been at the maternity home only since March 27, having previously worked in maternity homes and nursing homes at Malvern and Worcester. She is believed to be a native of Edinburgh.

Scotland Yard was called to help after a post-mortem examination had been made on Monday. "The results of the examination were enough to arouse suspicion," Supt. Spooner said. Other forensic scientists may be called to help to-day.

The inquest on Miss Bennett will be opened this morning in Stratford Town Hall before the South Warwickshire Coroner, Mr. F. S. Lodder.

Malvern Enquiries

Police enquiries were made yesterday at Malvern after it had been learned that a few weeks before moving to Stratford Miss Bennett worked at two nursing homes there. Worcestershire C.I.D. said that the enquiries there were routine.

While in Malvern Miss Bennett was not working as a midwife as she had not been registered with the Worcestershire County Council to practise as such.

Memorial Plaque Torn from Wall

Minister Keeps Secret of Confession by Two Men

A plaque in memory of an evangelist, which was torn from the wall of a shelter at Swansea in February, has been recovered.

The Rev. Leon Atkin, of St. Paul's Church, Swansea, said that two young men called on him on Monday and told him they wanted to confess that, while drunk, they took away the plaque, which was in memory of Tom Rees, a Swansea evangelist. They asked that their identity be kept secret, and offered to pay the expense of replacing the plaque.

Mr. Atkin said: "I decided to exercise my right as a minister of religion and withhold their identity."

As Mr. Atkin was giving the plaque to the treasurer of the Tom Rees Memorial Fund yesterday, two

On St. Valentine's Day **1945**, seventy-four-year-old resident of Lower Quinton, Charles Walton, set out for a day's work on Meon Hill, unaware it would be his last. His job that day was to continue planting a hedge for local farm owner, Albert Potter, of the Firs Farm.

At 6 pm that evening, Walton's niece, with whom he lived, returned home from work to find her uncle had not returned, which was unusual as he was always home before her. Edith Walton began to worry that something may have happened to him and called on her neighbour, Harry Beasley, to help search for him.

Together they set out for Potter's farm. On arrival at the spot where Charles was known to be working that day, they found his body. He had been savagely murdered; his trouncing hook was found embedded in his chest, a slash in the shape of a cross had been engraved into his chest and a pitchfork had been driven through his neck.

The local police constable, PC Lomasney, was called for and swiftly arrived at the scene, confirming that Charles was dead. He also discovered the deceased man's pockets were empty and his inexpensive tin pocket-watch was missing.

Due to the severity of the murder, Scotland Yard was called in to investigate.

In due course, Detective-Superintendent Robert Fabian arrived in Lower Quinton, but he found the villagers were reluctant to talk, and no evidence could be found against any person, so Fabian returned to London.

Years later, when questioned about the case, Fabian said he only ever had one suspect - the farmer, Potter. However, there was no concrete evidence to connect him to the murder.

All that is known for sure is that Potter was the last to see Charles alive on the day he died, and his fingerprints were found on the handle of Walton's pitch-fork.

Charles Walton is buried at

St Swithin's

1 Main Road

Lower Quinton

Stratford-Upon-Avon

CV37 8SG

Head Almost - Severed

A hedge cutter, aged about 75, was found dead early to-day in a ditch near Stratford-on-Avon, with his head almost severed from his body.

The man was later identified as Charles Walton (75), who lived with his niece at Upper Quinton, and for whom search was made when he failed to return home last night.

Report from the Gloucester Citizen 15 February 1945

KILLER LOVERS

John Butler, 62, was a lock keeper on the River Severn at Holt Fleet, Worcestershire. Up to her death in 1860, John was assisted in his duties by his wife, Francis. Shortly after her death, John employed a housekeeper, Catherine Gulliver. This soon developed into a romantic relationship, but it was a rocky one due to Butler's jealousy.

On 13 August 1864, Catherine went shopping and she complained to shopkeeper, Mrs Taylor, about the way Butler was treating her. She proceeded to the local pub for a glass of beer and bought some to take home with her. At 11 pm that evening Catherine went back to the pub complaining to Mrs Green, the wife of the landlord, that Butler had locked her out of the cottage. Mrs Green offered her a bed for the night but Catherine refused, in the belief, Butler would have calmed down and would let her back in. Mrs Green said that she would sit up until midnight and if there was any more trouble she was to return to her at the pub.

Shortly afterwards, Henry Thrupp saw Catherine walking along the towpath towards the cottage; he called out 'goodnight' to her. A little later, Mrs Green's daughter heard three screams ring out, coming from the direction of the cottage. The screams were also heard by the under lock keeper John and his wife Elizabeth who lived next door to Butler.

The following morning, Elizabeth saw Butler and asked him about the screams she and her husband heard the previous evening; he Butler replied they were from

Catherine. She had come home drunk, thrown the shopping around and stormed off in a temper. He had not seen her since.

For several days, people continued asking him about Catherine. Butler repeated the same story; he also suggested she was staying with friends in Worcester. However, people who were acquainted with Catherine knew she had no friends in that area. Rumours of her disappearance soon reached Rev John Gutney Rogers who was aware of the volatile relationship between the two. He confronted Butler about Catherine's disappearance but was not satisfied with his answer. Rodgers went straight to the police and reported his suspicion to Sergeant Matthews who was aware of the turbulent relationship between Catherine and John. Matthews had on occasion warned Butler to treat her in a better manner to which he promised he would.

With his suspicions aroused, Matthews ordered the river to be dredged. On 17 August, they pulled a fully clothed body of a woman from the water, close to where Butler worked. Surgeon Busigny was sent for. He identified the body as Catherine's, as he also knew her. There was clear evidence of violence on her body. At the post mortem, no water was found in her lungs, meaning she was dead before entering the water. Butler was immediately arrested and charged with the wilful murder of Catherine Gulliver; his only response was 'Oh, dear'.

On 12 December 1864, Butler appeared before Worcester Assizes. Found guilty, he was sentenced to hang. An appeal was launched on his behalf but this failed and he was executed on 5 January 1865.

On the following pages, you will see the census from 1885, and 1861, showing John Butler plus two newspaper reports on the case.

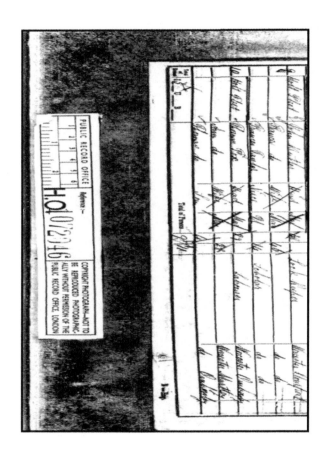

THE MURDER IN WORCESTERSHIRE.

Verdict of Wilful Murder.

The inquiry before the coroner into the death of Catherine Gulliver was resumed on Thursday afternoon, at Holt Fleet.

It will be remembered that the deceased was housekeeper to an old man named Butler, the keeper of the Holt Fleet lock on the River Severn, five miles from Worcester; that on the night of the 13th August they quarrelled; that a noise like the bleating of a sheep was heard by the neighbours late during the night, coming from a woman on the lock side, and who was calling some one "an old scamp and a villain;" that Gulliver was missed from her home next day, and that her body, bearing marks of violence, was found in the Severn, near to the lock, and within a few yards of Butler's house. He maintained a stolid indifference to all the inquiries as to where the woman had gone, and it was thought his intellect was impaired to some extent. Evidence was brought forward to show that a jealous feeling had existed between Butler and the deceased, that on one occasion he had threatened to drown her, and that the marks of violence on her head were most likely caused by blows. Since the inquest was adjourned the woman's bonnet, which she said Butler had torn from her head on the night of the quarrel, has been found by the police and identified.

At the adjourned inquest on Thursday some additional evidence was given by the woman Mary Green, the wife of the beer-house keeper, to whom the deceased complained of the old man's behaviour. Mrs. Green says that on the evening of the 15th inst., two days after the supposed murder, she went to Butler's house and asked him how he was. He replied, "Middling; I owe you 3d. for eggs." Witness said, "Yes, but I did not come up for that." He paid her, and then she asked him if he had heard anything of Mrs. Gulliver. He said, "No, but I suppose she has gone to see her friends, as she had been talking about doing so." Witness said she had got no friends, and Butler made her no answer, but looked up and sighed. She then said, "I doubt she's drowned; she's in the water." He kept silent, and she could get no answer at all from him. He seemed put about.

George Knight, a labourer, said that as he and a companion were passing by the lock-house about half-past five o'clock on the morning of the 14th they saw Butler standing at the mouth of the lock looking into the water, but as soon as he saw them he went into his own house and peeped through the door, as if he was watching them.

The coroner having summed up, the jury returned a verdict of "wilful murder" against the accused.

The Illustrated Usk Observer and Raglan Herald September 1864

SUSPECTED MURDER OF A WOMAN.

A case of, to say the least of it, very great suspicion, has just come to light at Holt Fleet, a picturesque village on the River Severn, a few miles from Worcester. The victim of what is supposed to be a brutal murder is a woman named Catherine Culliver, about 44 years of age, who had for about three years been living as housekeeper with a man named John Butler, lock-keeper at the Holt Fleet lock. It seems that Butler, who is a man possessing a little property, has lived on more than intimate terms with the woman, although their cohabitation was of a very unhappy nature. Jealousy is said to have crept in, and constant quarrels were the result. So frequent had brawls between them become that persons living next door took no notice of the violent screams of the woman in the dead of the night, although they seemed to come from the edge of the lock, and each fresh disturbance lessened the amount of attention paid to them by the neighbours. On Saturday night last a disturbance occurred, and on Sunday morning the woman was missed. Subsequent search for her led to the discovery of her dead body on Wednesday in the deep water immediately below the lock kept by Butler. The body was taken to an adjacent public house kept by Samuel Green, and Butler was apprehended, taken before Mr J. G. Watkins, a magistrate for that division of the county, and formally remanded, on a charge of suspected murder. He is a man of about 62 years of age, bearing a good character for steadiness and honesty, and has been in the service of the Severn Navigation Commissioners upwards of 20 years, as lock-keeper at Holt Fleet.—" Birmingham Post."

27 August 1864

Priscilla Brown was murdered on 14 May 1818, by her lover, John Gallop, after she confided to him that she was pregnant with his child. This would have been the third child born out of wedlock Priscilla; her first being her 8-year-old son, Charles, the second her daughter, Charlotte.

On the evening of the 14th May, Ann Loveridge, a neighbour of Priscilla, heard her call out, and then suddenly everything went quiet. Ann asked another neighbour, Elizabeth Rose if she had heard anything but she had not. After a quick search around the area, Loveridge decided it was nothing to worry about. A while later, a labourer by the name of Robert Lane, who knew Priscilla, was walking along, when he saw the body of a woman lying on a dung heap. On closer inspection, he recognized the body as being that of Pricilla. Thinking she'd had a fit, he tried to help her. When she failed to respond, Lane feared the worst and ran for help. He returned with Priscilla's brother and a neighbour, who carried the woman back to her house, and summoned a doctor.

Their worst fears were soon confirmed; she was dead, but worse news was to follow.

On examining her body, Dr Nott concluded that, due to marks around her neck, Priscilla had been strangled. He also confirmed she was pregnant.

The police were duly informed and soon their investigation into the murder of Priscilla Brown began. It was not long before they found their main suspect, namely John Gallop, who was rumoured to be the father of her unborn child. They also had several witnesses who had seen John walking towards Priscilla's cottage on the day of the murder. He was promptly arrested and charged with the murder of Priscilla Brown.

At his trial, Gallop pleaded not guilty and denied being the father of her unborn child. Among the witnesses to the events of that night, the police also called upon Priscilla's son, Charles, who testified that on the night of his mother's death, John had appeared at the cottage door where she had spoken to him. His mother then left the house and Charles didn't see her again until they brought her home dead. Throughout the trial, John disputed the testimony of the witnesses.

Finally, taking the stand himself, Gallop called the witnesses liars and said he had an alibi for that night, yet Gallop could not bring or name anyone to bear witness for him. It took the jury only a few minutes to find him 'Guilty'. On 27 July 1818, John Gallop was executed, still claiming his innocence.

Record of Priscilla Brown's death from the Dorset, Church of England Deaths and Burials 1813-2010

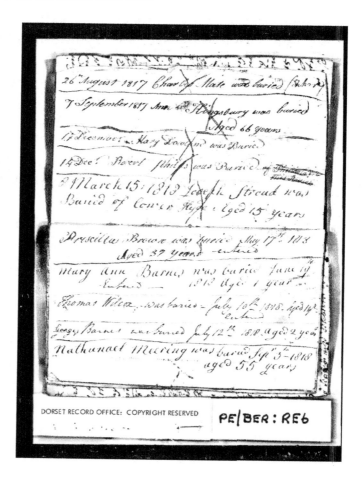

PE/BER: RE6

Thomas Tarver, aged 24 and Harriet Tarver, 21, of Chipping Campden had been married for just a little over a year, having married on 29 January 1834.

On December 11 1835, Harriet took the deadly decision to lace Thomas's breakfast of rice pudding with arsenic. When Thomas arrived at work that morning, he was taken ill with severe stomach pains and chronic vomiting. By 2 pm the same day, he was dead.

As Thomas was young and healthy, suspicion was immediately aroused into the cause of his death. The local authorities ordered a post-mortem and for the contents of his stomach to be examined. The examination revealed his stomach contained traces of arsenic, and Harriet was duly arrested for his murder.

Her guilt was never in question, as two witnesses confirmed she had recently brought two separate parcels of arsenic. After her trial, she was admitted to Gloucester Gaol and confessed to her crime. However, her motive for the crime never discovered. One theory was that she was having an affair, but this was never substantiated, so Harriet would go to her grave keeping her secret.

On Saturday 9 April 1836, Harriet Tarver was executed; aged just 21 she became the youngest woman to be hanged in Gloucestershire that century.

Prison record of Harriet Tarver

Below is the burial Record for James who was buried in the churchyard of the church where he was baptized and married before his untimely death

Page 101.

BURIALS in the Parish of *Chipping Campden* in the County of *Gloucester*				in the Year 1835
Name.	Abode.	When buried.	Age.	By whom the Ceremony was performed.
Sarah Jarvis No. 801.	*Campden*	*Dec 8*	*7 Month*	*D. Llewelly*
Thomas Turvor No. 802.	*Campden*	*Dec 16*	*24*	*D. Llewelly*
John Keyte	*Campden*	*Jan 2*	*59*	*D. Llewelly*

St James Church, Chipping Campden

KILLER IN THE FAMILY

Sidney Richard Russell was born in East Wellow, Hampshire, to Robert Russell, a miller, and his wife Maria Scutt, but for most of his life, he lived in Bere Regis, Dorset. Following his mother's death in 1873, his father Robert left him in the care of his grandparents, Richard and Sarah Scutt. His grandfather died in the early half of 1886, leaving Russell and Sarah Scutt, aged 79, living in the cottage. The 21-year-old gardener decided to join his uncle William Scott, in Australia.

On October 13 1886, just hours before he was due to leave, he went to the police station to report his grandmother had died during the night. PC George Bugby accompanied Russell back to the cottage, under the assumption she had been taken ill, and a doctor would have to attend. However, Russell said there was no need to fetch a doctor, confessing "The fact is that I have shot her." Entering the cottage, Bugby went upstairs to Sarah Scutt's bedroom where he found her in a corner of the room, dressed in her nightdress and surrounded by a pool of blood.

Bugby arrested Russell and cautioned him, but Russell had more to say: "I was drunk and did not know what I was doing," and "I and my grandmother had ale and mead together and she went to bed between nine and ten and then I drunk some raw spirits which overcame me."

At the inquest, it was revealed Sarah Scutt had been shot by her right ear; the bullet passing through her skull. Russell was committed for trial at Hampshire Assizes.

In the subsequent investigation performed by PC Bugby and Superintendent Feltham, they discovered Russell had visited an ironmongery owned by John Drew in Wareham on 12th October. He purchased a pistol and a box of 50 cartridges; he told Drew it was for shooting birds. Drew asked him if he knew how to use the gun; he said 'no', so he took Russell to the rear of the premises and demonstrated how to use the gun.

Furthermore, a neighbour, Mrs Sherren, reported that on the evening of the murder, Russell had taken aim at her with the gun and threatened her 'to mind her eye'. She rushed inside and the locked door, hearing a shot followed by two more.

Russell went to visit his employer, gardener Robert Farnham, at his home at midnight on the 13th of October. He told Farnham he wanted to say goodbye and he couldn't rest in his bed. Farnham asked Russell why he was troubled, but he replied it was nothing in particular, yet he was acting strangely, pacing back and forth around the room. Farnham tried to get rid of him saying he was trying to sleep, but Russell continued to pace up and down. He asked Farnham to go home with him but he refused.

A visit to his sister-in-law, Caroline Cozen, revealed he suffered from bouts of depression and at school had suffered from fits. Asked about his drinking habits she said she'd only ever seen him sober.

Sidney Russell's trial took place on 9 November 1886 at Winchester Castle, Hampshire, before Baron Huddleston. Dr Syms, superintendent of Dorset courts asylum, said on his examination of Russell, he found him to be 'weak of intelligent', and this was used as Russell's defence. Baron Huddleston was not impressed and had a few chosen words to say. The jury found him guilty but with a recommendation for mercy. He was sentenced to death. On November 24 he was reprieved and received a life sentence.

However, Sidney Russell did not survive long. He died from acute tuberculosis on 14 June 1888, still a prisoner in Chatham Prison Gillingham, Kent.

Sidney Russell's prison record can be seen on the next few pages.

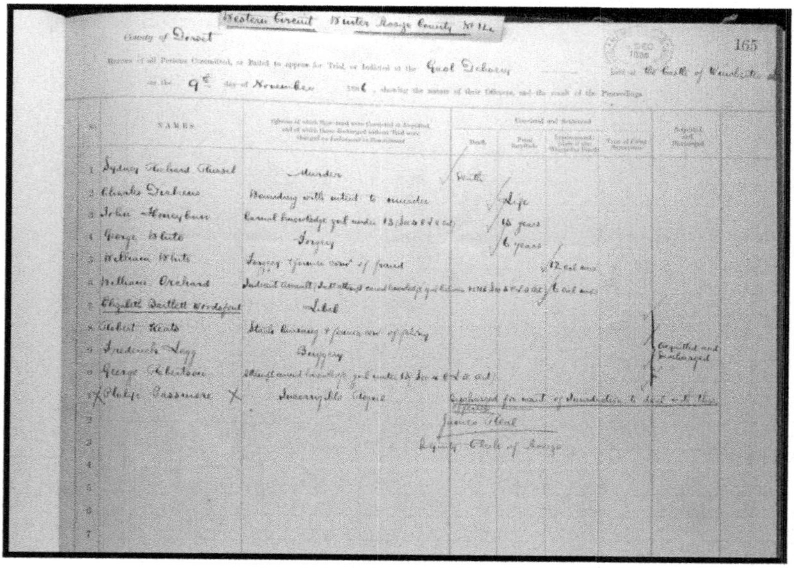

Western Circuit

County of Dorset

165

No.	NAMES	Offences	Death	Penal Servitude	Imprisonment	Acquitted and Discharged
1	Sydney Richard Russel	Murder	Death			
2	Charles Deabon	Wounding with intent to murder		Life		
3	John Honeybun	Carnal knowledge girl under 13		15 years		
4	George White	Forgery		6 years		
5	William White	Forgery & former conv of fraud			12 cal mos	
6	William Orchard	Indecent Assault			6 cal mos	
7	Elizabeth Bartlett Woodsford	Libel				
8	Albert Keats					Acquitted and Discharged
9	Frederick Legg	Buggery				Acquitted and Discharged
10	George Robertson	Attempt carnal knowledge girl under 13				Acquitted and Discharged
11	Philip Bassmore	Incorrigible Rogue				

James [illegible]

Deputy Clerk of Assize

Ann Cormel was murdered on 4 February 1707 by John Allan, Giles Hunt, Tom Dun, Thomas Symonds and Thomas Palmer.

Ann Cormel's death was not originally believed to be a homicide. There had been a fire at her home and it was believed that Ann had died in the blaze. When her body was recovered, there was found to be a large hole in her skull, however, no suspicions were aroused. It was believed that the hole was caused by a large beam falling on poor Ann's head. Consequently, Ann was buried in the local churchyard and there the story should have ended.

However, in November of 1707, another fire broke out. This time it was at the home of Mrs Ann Palmer (Mrs Palmer is named as Alice in some sources) in the village, of Upton Snodbury. This would bring Ann Cormel's true cause of death to come to light. One of Mrs Palmer's neighbours heard screaming and raised the alarm. Sadly, it was too late to save Mrs Palmer and her maid. They did, however, manage to pull Mrs Palmer's body from the burning house before it collapsed, and it was apparent that the injuries to her head had not been caused accidentally.

Suspicion soon fell on Mrs Palmer's son, John, whom it was claimed the deceased had told people she was afraid he would kill her. Suspicion was further aroused when he made a little attempt to find his mother's killer.

The breakthrough came when the vicar of Upton Snodbury came forward and told the Worcester magistrate that, in the early hours of the 8th November; Giles Hunt had been seen going into his brother's home with blood on his sleeves and trousers.

Hunt was quickly apprehended but explained that the blood was from a fight and gave an alibi for his movements that evening, which turned out to be false. A search of his home found items engraved with the initials A.P. When confronted with the evidence, Hunt confessed to the crime and freely named his associates, who are named above, including Mrs Palmer's son. After the second search of his home, a silver box was found which was identified as belonging to Ann Cormel.

When confronted with the box, Hunt also confessed to robbing and killing Ann Cormel and named his accomplice as the same man who had robbed and killed Mrs Palmer. Giles Hunt turned Queen's evidence and was pardoned while the others were found guilty and hanged.

Mary Blandy was born in 1729, the only child of Francis Blandy, an attorney and town clerk of Henley-on-Thames in Oxfordshire, and his wife, Anne. The family home was 29 Hart Street in the town centre.

Francis unwisely advertised a dowry of £10,000 for the man who would become Mary's husband. The Honourable Captain William Henry Cranstoun who was in the army and the son of a Scottish nobleman, and some twenty years Mary's senior, became her accepted suitor in 1746. Subsequently, Francis began having suspicions about Cranstoun. He had every right to be to because there was a big obstacle in the way of William marrying Mary. William was already married to Anne Murray who he had wed in 1745. He also had a child back in Scotland.

Cranstoun went back to Scotland in an attempt to dissolve his marriage. While there he sent letters and parcels to Mary. The packages contained white powders which he claimed were a love potion that would change her father's mind about their marriage. Mary put the powder in Francis's tea and gruel, which made him ill, and after some months, he died on 14 August 1751. Before he died, Francis Blandy confided to his doctor that he thought he was being poisoned by his daughter.

Mary was immediately confined to her room; however, on finding the door open, she slipped out and went for a walk around Henley. The townsfolk were not happy and chased her over the bridge into Remenham where she took refuge with her friend, Mrs Davis, the landlady of the 'Little Angel', before being taken back into custody.

Blandy was tried at Oxford, on 3 March 1752, convicted upon strong evidence, including that of her father's physician, Anthony Addington. She was **executed** on 6 April 1752, her last request being that, for the sake of decency, she should not be hoisted too high.

As for William Cranstoun, he disappeared but he did not live long and died on 2nd December 1752.

Mary Blandy was buried next to her parents in St Mary's churchyard, Henley on Thames, Oxfordshire.

Burial record for, Francis Blandy, with an added note saying he was poisoned by his only child, Mary Blandy.

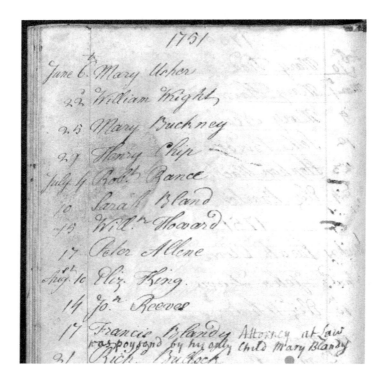

Burial record for Mary Blandy, with an added note saying she was executed for poisoning her father Francis Blandy.

Sarah Freeman (Dimond) was born in 1816, in the county of Shapwick, Somerset, one of ten children born to Charles and Mary Dimond. She was described as an unruly child.

By the time of her marriage to Henry Freeman, on 16 May 1841, in the Holy Trinity Church, Bridgwater, Somerset, she had two illegitimate children, none of whom were Henry's. Accounts recall a clergyman paid Harry to marry Sarah, after having had an affair with her.

In 1843, Sarah's illegitimate son, James, aged 7, started experiencing extreme stomach pains and vomiting. The cause was thought to be cholera. He passed away and was buried in the Blessed Virgin Mary churchyard, Ashcott. On the 27 December of the same year, Sarah's husband, Henry, also died after experiencing similar symptoms. Sarah collected money from the life insurance policy her husband had taken out and immediately left the area.

A year later with no money, she reappeared at the home of her mother Mary and her brother Charles Dimond. Her brother wasn't happy and told her she was not welcome, but under the circumstances, she could stay with them. Yet another death was inflicted upon Sarah's family. On December 9 1844, Sarah's mother Mary, aged 72, began suffering the same symptoms as Sarah's son and husband. She died on December 14 1844. On Boxing Day 1844, Charles Dimond began having stomach pains and vomiting: he died December 31 1844.

Suspicion was aroused over the death of a healthy man, and an autopsy was ordered. Doctors found traces of arsenic in his intestines and liver. Immediately the bodies of Sarah's mother, son and husband were ordered to be exhumed. During the post-mortem examinations, the doctors found arsenic in all three bodies.

Sarah Freeman was charged with four murders but was only tried for the murder of her brother Charles. She appeared at the Somerset Lent Assize in Taunton before Mr Justice Coleridge on April 5 1845. Her defence explained to the jury that they had to be satisfied that arsenic had indeed been the cause of death and if they, were absolutely positive Sarah had administered it. He also tried to persuade the jury that there was no evidence of motive or malice in the killing and that there was at least reasonable doubt to Sarah's guilt.

However it was established from witness testimony, Sarah had on 9 December 1844 (the day Sarah's mother became ill) visited a Bridgwater chemist and bought a three-penny bottle of arsenic, claiming she needed it to kill rats. It took the jury just 15 minutes to return a guilty verdict, and for Judge Justice Coleridge to pass the death sentence.

In the condemned cell, she intimated her brother John Dimond was the real culprit and she was innocent as a lamb. She went to the gallows on April 23 still maintaining her innocence.

THE SOMERSETSHIRE MURDERS.

At half-past 11 o'clock on Friday morning the coroner and jury met at Shapwick, and proceeded with the adjourned inquest upon the body of the illegitimate child of Sarah Freeman, named James Dimond, aged 7 years, whose body was exhumed on Saturday last.

A great deal of evidence was gone into.

The Coroner then summed up the evidence, and the jury returned a verdict of "Wilful Murder against Sarah Freeman."

The jury having recorded their verdict in the case of the son, the coroner proceeded with the adjourned inquest on the body of the husband, Henry Freeman, who died on the 27th of December, 1843, was buried in Shapwick church-yard on the 2d of January, 1844, and disinterred for the purpose of examination January 11, 1845. The first witness called was,

Mr. William Herapath, who deposed to the exhumation of the body of the deceased, Henry Freeman. The body was entire. On opening it, the intestinal canal was also entire, except the colon, the upper surface of which was decomposed. On examination he found the mucous coat of the interior of the stomach was highly inflamed over its whole surface, but more particularly in two or three places. The surface of several parts of the intestines was in the same state—these had all lost their fluid and were compacted into one mass, from which he could dissect the intestines very readily; they had, therefore, been particularly preserved. Mr. Herapath then again described the processes which he had used, which were the same as in the former cases, and produced arsenic in its several forms. He added,—I have no doubt, from my experiments, that arsenic has been the cause of death. Other evidence was adduced.

The Coroner then summed up the evidence, and

The jury returned a verdict of "Wilful murder against Sarah Freeman.'

The Welshman 24 January 1845

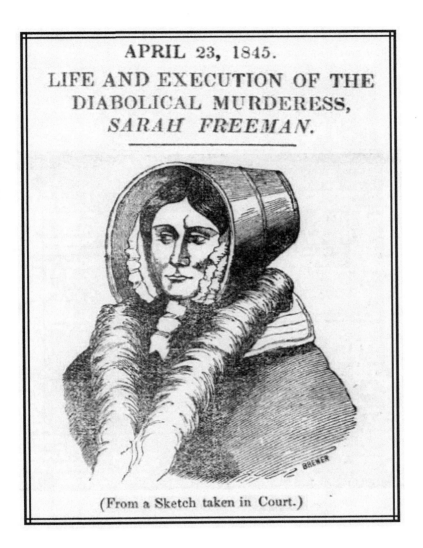

APRIL 23, 1845.

LIFE AND EXECUTION OF THE DIABOLICAL MURDERESS, *SARAH FREEMAN.*

(From a Sketch taken in Court.)

Burial records of Mary and Charles Dimond. The cause of death, poison, is written next to their names.

Burial for James Dimond and Henry Freeman; again, poison is noted next to the names.

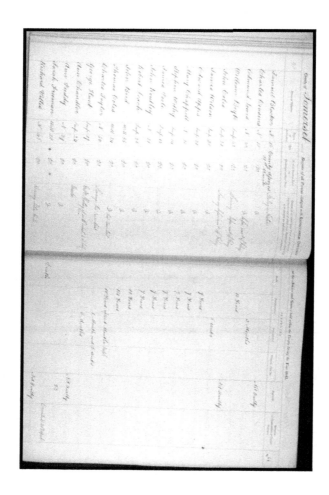

Sarah Freeman (Dimond) prison record

On 4 September 1894, the bodies of Rebecca Hartland, aged 57, and her youngest son, George aged 13, were found at No.303 Lower High Street, Cheltenham. Both had been murdered by Rebecca's husband Job Hartland, aged 60, a greengrocer at the above address.

Job was a drunk who frequently threatened his wife with violence, to the extent that the older children of Rebecca and Job had all left home by 1894, leaving Rebecca and young George alone with Job. On the Friday before their deaths, Rebecca woke during the night to find Job standing over her holding a hatchet. She refused to stay another night in the house with him and spent the next two nights staying with her daughter.

However, on Monday the 3rd September, against the advice given to her, she returned home to attend to the family's grocery business and slept there instead of returning to her daughter's home. The next morning her body was found in her bed, alongside the body of her son, George. Job had attacked them, firstly with a coal hammer, beating them about the head, before using a butcher's knife which nearly severed his wife's head. He slit the throat of his son.

He then calmly went to a nearby public house where he confessed to murdering two people.

At the Gloucestershire Assizes he was convicted of murder and sentenced to death, but with a recommendation of mercy from the Judge, despite the brutality of the crime.

A petition was soon launched to save his life, citing at the time of the crime, he was heavily under the influence of drink and oblivious of his behaviour. The petition was signed by local businessmen and members of the clergy. He also received the support of the Judge and the jury from his trial. The petition was a success and his sentence was commuted to life in prison.

Job spent the last two years of his life in HMP Portsmouth.

Page 86

BURIALS in the Parish of _Portland_ in the County of _Dorset_ in the year One thousand eight hundred and _Ninety Six_.

Name.	Abode.	When buried.	Age.	By whom the Ceremony was performed.
Walter Victor Cattel No. 681	Chesil	Dec 18	18 months	J M Beazor Rector
Thomas Elcall No. 682	King Street	Dec 19	86 years	M Beazor Rector
Frederick Mayes No. 683	Grove	Dec 19	13 months	J M Beazor Rector
Beatrice Amy Peeter No. 684	11 Queen's Row	Dec 21	2 months	M Olley vicar S. John Portland
Jno Hartland No. 685	Portland Prison	Dec 22	62 years	J Sneigh Vicar St Peter Portland
Dorothy Mackenzie No. 686	Fortuneswell	Dec 26	6 days	✗
John Thomas Winter Russell No. 687	Spring Gardens	Dec 28	69 years	M Beazor Rector
Jane Willis No. 688	Reforne	Dec 29	75 years	M Beazor Rector

PE/PTD: RE 4/3

HORRIBLE TRAGEDY AT CHELTENHAM.

A Cheltenham correspondent says :—A green-grocer named Hartland on Tuesday murdered his wife and son, while they were in bed, by cutting their throats. Hartland had recently given way to drink, and frequently threatened his wife, but these threats were not regarded seriously until last Friday, when he held a chopper over Mrs Hartland. In consequence of this she did not sleep at home on Saturday and Sunday nights. On Monday night, however, she returned home, although advised not to do so, and during the night or early on Tuesday her life and that of her son were taken. After the deed, the man went to a public-house and said that he had killed his wife and child. He was afterwards taken into custody by the police.

PRISONER BEFORE THE MAGISTRATES.

At Cheltenham Police-court on Tuesday Job Hartland, aged 60, greengrocer, High-street, Cheltenham, was charged with the wilful murder of his wife, Rebecca Hartland, aged 57, and his youngest son, aged 13. The prisoner, a short, thickset man, with a receding forehead, was assisted into the dock and trembled violently. Only formal evidence was given, and the prisoner was remanded till Wednesday next.

24 November 1894 The Western Mail

Overview of Cheltenham cemetery

GREED

Herbert Burrows was a 23-year-old serving probationary constable, with the Worcester constabulary, when he was condemned to death for the murders of Ernest Laight aged 31, his wife Doris, 30 and their 2-year-old son Robert.

Ernest was the landlord of the Garibaldi Inn on Wylds Lane. Burrows lived opposite the pub. On the evening of 27 November 1925, Burrows, unusually, stayed on after closing time. After the last drinkers left, Burrows and Ernest were left alone at the bar. Burrows pulled out a gun and shot Ernest. When Doris heard a bang, she came to investigate and was also shot. He then went upstairs and battered Robert to death; afraid his crying may attract attention. Returning downstairs, he removed the evening's takings from the till, yet he did not hurt the Laight's daughter Joan.

The murders weren't discovered until the following morning, by the cleaner.

Meanwhile, Burrows carried on as normal and the following morning he was back on duty. For whatever reason, he asked a fellow officer, PC Devey, if he had heard anything about a shooting at the Garibaldi Inn. At that moment in time, no one had reported a crime, so he answered 'no'. When news did break of the shooting, Burrows had clearly implicated himself with his question to Devey.

PC Devey reported the conversation to his senior officers. On a search of Burrows' lodgings, they found the gun and the stolen money. Confronted with the facts, he confessed to the murders and the robbery.

The trial of Herbert Burrows took place at Worcester on 27 January 1926, before Mr Justice Sankey. He was found guilty and sentenced to hang. Burrows chose not to appeal, and his execution took place within the walls of Gloucester Prison on Wednesday 17th February, performed by Thomas Pierrepoint and assisted by Robert Baxter.

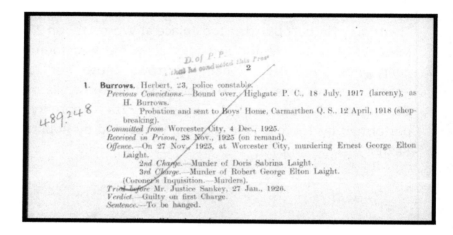

Herbert Burrows prison record, recording his sentence of death; also his previous convictions.

Francois Jacques Rens aged 64 (known locally as Francis James Rens), was a French gentleman, who lived and worked in Stow on the Wold, Gloucestershire. On the evening of Friday 10 March 1834, like most evenings, Rens took a walk around the town. However, on this particular night, he was attacked and robbed of his gold watch and purse. He was also severely beaten about the head and left for dead. Rens was only ninety yards from the George Inn where he lived. (The George Inn no longer exists; in its place stands the local police station.)

Samuel Harris who was returning from tending to horses, found Rens lying in the road bleeding, after hearing a groan. Harris reported his findings at the George Inn, whereupon, the ostler Stephen and gamekeeper Charles Shepherd returned to the body with him, at which point the body was identified as belonging to Francois. The body was returned to his lodgings. An examination by a local surgeon, George Bulley Haywood, revealed Rens had several wounds to the head, of which one was so severe, his brain could be seen. He survived approximately four hours after the attack.

Two local men were soon the main suspects; the first was John Clifford, a stonemason, whose misfortune it was to be seen on the night of the murder carrying a heavy wooden stick, and appeared to have what was blood on his trousers. The second, Richard Cox, a sawyer, had the misfortune of having no alibi for the time of the murder and was a known poacher. Both men were arrested within a week of the murder and held at Gloucester gaol, charged with murder. With no evidence against them, the case was thrown out of court due to a lack of evidence.

Several months passed until a significant event occurred on September 19 1834. Edwin Jeffrey, a 21-year-old labourer employed by Mr Ellis, a butcher and farmer of Stow, took a gold watch for repair to a gentleman called George Thornton of Stow. He in turn took some of the watch components to a George Payne, watchmaker, who recognised them as belonging to Rens's watch. Jeffrey was soon apprehended, and after a few days, in custody (28 September 1834) he made a full confession to Rev R W Ford, a local magistrate. He said he acted alone in the crime and had taken his master's stick and stuck Rens about the head.

His motivation was stealing the gold watch belonging to Rens. After striking the victim and taking the watch, Jeffrey concealed it in a nearby garden. He then waited three days before retrieving it. Jeffery then hid the watch in a wall and covered it in hay. A month passed and he began wearing the watch and made sure he hid it from view when checking the time. After another six months, the watch stopped working properly; the rest as they say is history.

Jeffrey pleaded guilty to the charge but changed his plea on the advice of the judge who told him it wasn't in his best interest to plead guilty. However, he was still found guilty and was **executed** on 15 April 1835.

Francois Jacques Rens will

STOW-ON-THE-WOLD.—HIGHWAY ROBBERY AND MURDER.—
Great sensation and alarm have been excited in this town and all
the neighbouring country, in consequence of a diabolical instance
of highway robbery and murder (crimes almost unknown in this
part of the country), which was perpetrated on Monday evening
last, on the person of Mr. Rens, a gentleman of amiable dispo-
sition, and highly respected by all who knew him. It appears
Mr. Rens was returning home on the evening in question, after
a walk—and about half-past seven in the evening had reached
the horsepool, immediately adjoining Stow, on the Moreton road.
He was there seized and held by two men, while a third robbed
him of his watch and purse. The miscreants having accomplished this crime, immediately proceeded to the work of murder,
but with what weapons their infernal purpose was effected, has
not, we believe, been ascertained. When the unfortunate gentleman was found, his skull was dreadfully fractured—nearly all
his teeth beaten in—and his face horribly maimed and disfigured.
In this miserable condition, he was first seen by a man who went
to the pool to water his horse; and who was attracted to the spot
by the sound of deep groans. At that time Mr. Rens was just
able to relate, in broken accents, the story of his murder—after
which he was taken home in a state of insensibility, and continued to breathe until about eleven o'clock the same night, when
he expired. A reward of two hundred pounds has been offered
for the apprehension of the murderers. The watch is a double
gold case repeater, and Mr. Rens was supposed to have a sum of
money about him at the time of the robbery, in a brown silk
purse. Since writing the above, we have been informed that Mr.
Rens was of French extraction, and agent to — Pole, Esq., of
Wick Hill, for the Provident Bank in Stow.—On the previous
Thursday evening, a gentleman, while returning from Northleach
to Bourton-on-the-Water on horseback (near the place where the
murder was afterwards committed), was attacked by a man who
aimed a blow at his head with a large stick: the blow fortunately
struck the horse, which made the animal gallop off at full speed,
not stopping till he got home.—*Cheltenham Chronicle*.

Name.	Abode.	When buried.	Age.	By whom the Ceremony was performed.
Anne Cosier No. 605	Stow	Feby 25	68 years	B. Varason Rector
William John Bartlett No. 606	Stow	March 10th	7 months	B. Varason Rector
John Fox No. 607	Moreton in Marsh	March 12th	29 years	B. Varason Rector
Francis James Rens No. 608	Stow	March 14th	64 years	B. Varason Rector

BURIALS in the Parish of Stow on the Wold in the County of Gloucester in the Year 1834

[Page 76]

Burial record for Francois Jacques Rens

The police station where the George Inn once stood.

The lane Francois Jacques Rens walked down on that fatal night.

Around eight pm, on the evening of the 7 November 1820, William Hiron, a farmer from the village of Alveston in Warwickshire, was on his way home from Warwick where he had been voting in the county election. As he approached the Littleham Bridge he was attacked by four assailants, namely Nathaniel Quiney, Henry Adams, Samuel Sidney and Thomas Heytrey (recall Thomas was the brother of Ann Heytrey).

Quiney was a married father-of-seven from Stratford and worked with horses; Adams was 35 and worked with horses, he also was married with six children; Sidney was a blacksmith, married with no children, and Heytrey was 24, single and a blacksmith.

The four had been laying in wait for an opportunity to rob to commit robbery. As William approached their hiding place, they pulled him from his horse using a large hook attached to a pole, which they had made especially for the purpose. Adams later confessed it was he who dragged William from his horse. They then brutally bludgeoned him, leaving him for dead. Sidney would later confess that it was he who delivered the final blows to William after the others had walked away. The four made off with three one-pound notes, some coins and a pocketbook.

Badly beaten and with a fractured skull, William managed to crawl a small distance before he ended up in a ditch, where he was found the next morning; but his injuries were so severe that he died two days later. Henry Hiron, William's brother, and Mr Greenway who were both executives of Henry's will offered a reward for the capture of these responsible for the murder.

The parish constable, John Ashfield, had suspicions of who the four were and went in search of Thomas Heytrey. He found him and made the arrest. Thomas denied all knowledge of the crime. He was questioned about his whereabouts on the night of the murder but gave no satisfactory answer, he was then asked his whereabouts when he had heard about the murder. Firstly, he claimed he was at work when he heard about it, he then claimed he was at home.

At this point, events took a strange turn. Ashfield allowed Mr Greenway into the room with them. He brandished a wad of notes and suggested to Thomas that the money and a pardon could be his if he named his accomplices. He caved in and told Ashfield the whole story and named the others involved in the murder. Ashfield went to Thomas's lodgings to confirm he wasn't home at the time of the murder. He searched Thomas's room and found several pounds notes: more money than a penniless blacksmith should have. By morning, all four were remanded in custody. The local magistrate then proceeded to interview the accused. This took place at the Falcon Inn. Meanwhile, the four were allowed to drink strong ale and by the time of the interview, all were in a drunken state, and readily confessed to the crime.

The four appeared before the Honourable Sir John Richardson Knight, at the Warwickshire Lent Assizes, 1821. They tried to explain they were drunk when they confessed and that bribery had been involved, but the pleas were dismissed. All four were found guilty and sentenced to hang. They were all executed at Warwick Gaol on April 14 1821, and their bodies sent for dissection.

While Henry Adams was in prison, his wife died in childbirth leaving their children orphans.

This was not the end of the story. An indent of William Hiron's head was left in the ditch he had crawled into to rest his head. After numerous attempts to fill the hole, it reappeared within a few hours. The indent became known as "Hiron's Hole" and most people avoided the area after dark.

This continued for a long time until an elderly lady admitted the truth. William Hiron was a popular employer, so his former employees used to remove the hole fillings whilst going to and from work, to keep it as a kind of memorial.

No matter how often and with what, it was filled in. In time this stopped as the workers retired and died.

William Hiron is buried in the old church in Alveston, where a memorial tablet records the tragic event.

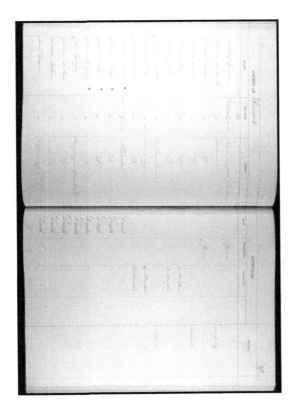

Prison record for Nathaniel Quiney, Henry Adams, Samuel Sidney and Thomas Heytrey

INSANITY

Edward Smart, also known as Saunders, was a troubled man. He was tried at Aylesbury for arson on 10 March 1865 and sentenced to six years penal servitude. He was released on 10 March 1870, and in August of the same year, he was tried again for arson. On this occasion, he was sentenced to ten years penal servitude. When he was released from prison in January 1879, he went to stay with his aunt, Julia Short, of Cambridge Street, in Totterdown, Bristol.

On the morning of Wednesday, April 2 1879, he left his aunt's house taking with him a razor, a hammer and two knives, belonging to his aunt's husband. He started walking towards Thornbury, where he saw two young girls standing outside the gate of Thornbury Castle. Edward made up his mind to murder them but, as he approached them, he noticed some people nearby, so he carried on walking.

When Edward reached Morton (a part of Thornbury), he stopped at the home of a Mr Penduck and asked a woman there for a drink of water. He again had the impulse to kill, but several children were playing nearby and he thought they might raise the alarm, so he continued.

Soon afterwards, he met Lucy Derrick. Lucy was aged between 32 and 37 (no one was quite sure she of her age), and was from Yatton, in Somerset.

She was on her way to meet her lover, Jacob Needs. Jacob was in the militia and had travelled to Gloucester for training. She told him she would follow him there and find employment and lodging.

Lucy left Yatton on Tuesday, April 1 1879, and reached Thornbury the following morning where she stopped at the Boar's Head for a glass of beer.

The publican later described her as respectably dressed and well-spoken. She had told him she had been living with her mother in law but was now on her way to join her husband who had found work in Gloucester. Lucy fell asleep before she had finished her glass of beer and the landlord let her rest there for a couple of hours.

After her stop, Lucy continued her journey. Unfortunately, she came across Edward Smart, and this time no one was around to help her. He was discovered sitting next to Lucy's body beside the road and was arrested after telling the person who found him that he had cut her throat. The post-mortem was performed by Thomas Henry Taylor, a surgeon from Thornbury. It revealed Lucy had been struck on the head five times with a hammer and her throat was almost severed to the spine. Taylor concluded the post mortem by saying it appeared the knife was not sharp enough and the accused had finished the job with a razor. Her body was identified by her, uncle, William Cooksley, a labourer from Blagdon, who appeared to have been her only living relative.

Lucy Derrick was buried on 8 April 1879, in St Mary's Churchyard, Thornbury

Edward was tried at Worcester Assize on 23 April 1879, and the only motive he could suggest for the murder was that he wanted to kill a woman, any woman! His execution took place on Monday 12 May and was performed by hangman, William Marwood.

THE THORNBURY MURDER.
EXECUTION OF THE CULPRIT.

Edward Smart, who was convicted at the Worcester Assizes of the murder of Lucy Derrick, at Thornbury, was executed at Gloucester on Monday morning. The deed for which the convict suffered was almost unique in the history of crime. He had led a dissolute life, and, according to his own statement, having grown completely tired of his existence, resolved to murder some one in order that he himself might be dismissed from the world by the hand of the executioner. He further stated that on the day of the murder he armed himself with a long knife for the specific purpose of carrying out his determination. He first called, as he alleged, at the cottage of a poor woman near Bristol, and decided to kill her while she was giving him the cup of water he had begged of her, but a group of children suddenly gathered round the door and his purpose was for the moment thwarted. A second design in respect of two little children was similarly frustrated. Soon afterwards, however, he met the unfortunate deceased, a domestic servant, on the highway, and he thereupon set upon her, and deliberately cut her throat from ear to ear. About an hour later Smart was seen by a passing traveller sitting near the body of his victim, and he at once acknowledged the crime, and stated his reason for its commission. During the trial the culprit displayed the utmost unconcern, and after his condemnation he maintained the same stolid and indifferent demeanour; indeed, he preserved it to the last. He slept well, and walked very quietly to the scaffold yesterday morning, apparently being perfectly unconcerned as to his fate. He remained silent while upon the scaffold, and exhibited no signs of fear. Upon the bolt being drawn, the condemned man struggled convulsively for a minute or two, and then expired. Marwood was the executioner.

The Monmouthshire Merlin and South Wales Advertiser May 1879

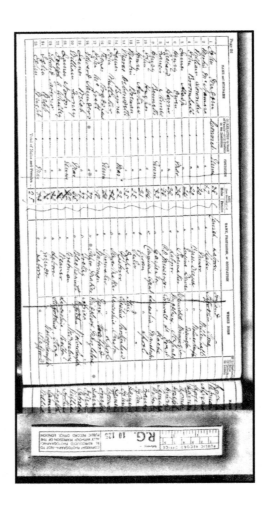

Prison census 1871 for Edward Smart also known as Saunders

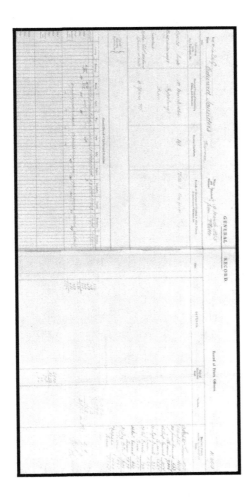

Edward Smart / Saunders prison record 1865

Edward Smart / Saunders prison record 1870

On the Wednesday evening of 15 September 1875, Ann Tennant left home to buy a loaf of bread, for her husband's tea, from a nearby bakery. She was never to return, for on her journey home James Haywood, a farmhand who had just finished his harvest work in a nearby field, set about her with his pitch-fork

Haywood inflicted several horrible wounds upon Mrs Tennant's body, yet throughout the entire attack, he never uttered a single word. A nearby farmer by the name of John Taylor tried to stop the murderous attack but sadly Mrs Tennant died from her injuries.

When Haywood was asked why he would do such a terrible and wicked thing he replied that Ann Tenant and several women villagers were witches and he was under their influence. He believed that killing them would break the spell they had over him.

On 17th September, an inquest was held at the Red Lion Inn, Long Compton, where a verdict of murder was brought against Haywood.

Brought to trial on 14 December 1875 at Warwick Crown Court, he was found not guilty on the grounds of insanity, ending his days in Broadmoor Criminal Lunatic Asylum where he died in 1890, aged 59.

A BEWITCHED FARM LABOURER.

A farm labourer named Hayward has been committed for trial to the next Warwick Assizes on a charge of wilfully murdering Ann Tennant, the wife of a pig dealer at Long Compton. It appeared that the prisoner was returning from work when, meeting the deceased, he deliberately ran up to her, and with a pitchfork he was carrying stabbed her several times in both legs, and afterwards commenced beating her about the head with the handle of the fork. The woman died in about three hours. On being taken into custody, the prisoner stated to the constable, "I hope she is dead; it's no odds about it; she was an old witch, and there are fifteen more in the village; I'll serve them the same; I'll kill them all. I was three hours in a bean-field the other day, and could not work, for they were witching me." Several of the witnesses deposed to the accused labouring under the delusion that he was haunted by witches, but in other respects he was perfectly rational, and had been employed from a boy by the various farmers of the village as a labourer.

A report on the attack from the South Wales Daily News 20 September 1875

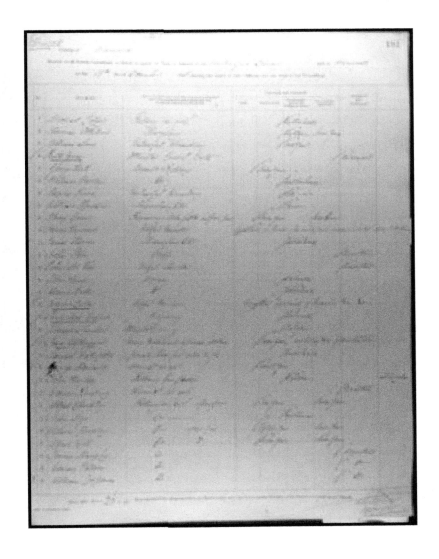

The 1881 census for Broadmoor Criminal lunatic asylum

Enoch Wadley was born in 1861, to James and Hannah Wadley of Much Marcel, Herefordshire. At the age of seventeen, he enlisted as a Private in the 2nd Gloucestershire Regiment. In January 1887, while severing in Ahmednuggur, India, he started displaying erratic behaviour. Mr K M O'Callighan, an army surgeon, drew up a certificate proclaiming Wadley was insane; the certificate was countersigned by the senior surgeon. In March 1887 he was invalided home to Netley Hospital on an Army certificate that stated he had been of unsound mind when in India, suffering from dementia, and had been eccentric for months, with supposed suicidal tendencies. On 7 June 1887, Wadley was released from Netley Hospital and discharged from the Army as someone who was once affected with insanity and sent home to his family in Kempley Gloucestershire.

On 15 June 1887, 27-year-old Wadley, having only been sent home eight days earlier murdered 18-year-old Elizabeth Hannah Evans.

Elizabeth was born in 1869, to Samuel Evans, a farm labourer from Kempley, and his wife Eliza Evans.

Wadley had gone to visit his sister-in-law, Elizabeth, who was working in nearby fields on Bickerton Court Farm with Elizabeth Evans. During his visit, he asked his sister-in-law did she think Elizabeth Evans loved him, as he had feelings for her.

When the women finished work for the day, Wadley told his sister-in-law that he was going to walk a little way with Elizabeth.

A little later, Arthur Dyer of Bickerton Court Farm who was tending to his sheep heard cries of distress and ran towards the sounds. He found Elizabeth on the side of the road covered with blood, and her clothes disarranged. She begged him to rub her legs as they were cold and she also asked him to pray for her because she was dying. After praying with her, he went to fetch her father. Elizabeth told her father she was dying and added Enoch Wadley was responsible. She was taken home and died there a few minutes later.

The doctor who examined her body found 38 wounds to her back, breasts and arms. He also believed she had been raped.

Meanwhile, Wadley was already in custody. He had made a public nuisance of himself, by giving away his purse containing £10 to a stranger. He threw his blood-stained coat and waistcoat into a cottage garden and was shouting out along the streets of Dymock, until the village constable locked him up to prevent further disturbance to the peace. While in custody, information of the murder reached the station and he was duly charged with murder.

Wadley's first trial took place on 15 July at Gloucester Summer Assize's before Baron Huddleston. His defence entered a plea of insanity, but Dr Oscar Clark of Gloucester prison believed him to be of sound mind at the time of the murder. The jury could not reach a verdict, saying although they agreed he committed the murder they could not agree on his mental state. A retrial was ordered.

On 22 October 1887, he wrote a letter to Elizabeth's parents to whom he gave a detailed account of how he committed the murder. He stated that when she resisted his advances and threatened to report him, he admitted he flew into a passion and caused her harm. The second trial was deferred so additional medical evidence could be obtained.

When the second trial finally took place on 11 November 1887, Wadley went before Mr Justice Hawkins. Again his sanity was brought into question, however, the jury had no problems this time and he was found guilty of murder and sentenced to hang.

Enoch Wadley was **executed** on Monday 28 November 1887 by James Berry.

THE SUPPOSED MURDER OF A GIRL NEAR LEDBURY.

On Wednesday evening (as briefly reported in the *Echo* last night) a young woman named Hannah Evans (19), residing at Kempley, was brutally murdered, it is alleged, by a pensioner named Wadley (27), residing in the same village. The girl had been at work with other women weeding in a field in an adjoining parish, and during the afternoon the man had proceeded to the field, and had tea with them. On leaving work at six o'clock the man accompanied the girl towards her home. They had not proceeded far when her employer heard loud cries. He proceeded in the direction of the noise, and found the poor girl lying in a pool of blood in a ditch by the road side, she having been stabbed in several places in the chest. Her clothing, too, was disarranged. When questioned, she said Wadley had done it. She was removed at once to her father's house, but died on the way thither. Information was given to the police, and Wadley was arrested. He was brought before the magistrates at Newent, yesterday, and remanded pending the inquest, which is to be held to-day at Kempley. It appears that Wadley was discharged from the army a week ago, on the ground of being medically unfit. He had served abroad seven years, in the second battalion of the Gloucestershire Regiment. Since his return he had resided with his father at Much Marche. The only cause known for the murder is the girl's refusal to accept him as her lover.

South Wales Echo 17 June 1887

EXECUTION OF THE CULPRIT THIS MORNING.

At 8 o'clock this morning, Enoch Wadley, 27, a discharged soldier, was executed in Gloucester gaol for the murder of Hannah Evans, a girl 18 years, of age at Kempley, near Ledbury, on the 13th June last. Wadley was courting the girl, and on the day named, whilst taking her home, suggested impropriety. His proposal being met with indignant refusal, he stabbed her to death, inflicting over 30 horrible wounds. At the trial insanity was set up as the defence, the prisoner, whilst in the army, having been declared insane, and subsequently discharged unfit for service. The jury unhesitatingly found him guilty. He spent his remaining days quite resigned to his fate. On the scaffold he was cool and required no assistance. Berry gave a drop of 5 feet 6 inches, and death appeared to have been instantaneous. The culprit repeated the responses of the burial service, and beseeched the Lord to receive his spirit.

South Wales Echo 28 1887

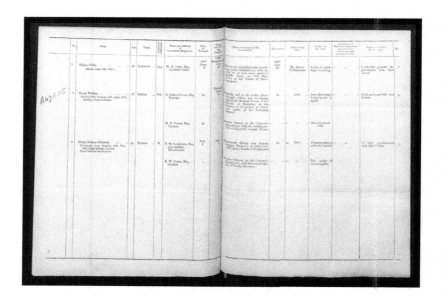

Prison record

Prison record

THE CAINES FAMILY

We bring the book to a close, by taking a brief look at the criminal history of two generations of the Caines family of Bitton, Gloucestershire.

Benjamin Caines (senior 1757-1824) also spelt Caines and Ann Cool (died 1833) had, nine children: six sons and three daughters. Of the six sons, two were **executed** for burglary and the other four were sentenced to transportation for theft, picking pockets and highway robbery.

Two of their daughters co-habited with six different men, five of whom were transported.

One grandson was **executed** while three others were transported.

On the next page, you will see a baptism record for three of the Caines children.

Page 14.

BAPTISMS solemnized in the Parish of _Bitton_
in the County of _Gloucester_ in the Year 18 45

When Baptized.	Child's Christian Name.	Parents' Names. Christian.	Surname.	Abode.	Quality, Trade, or Profession.	By whom the Ceremony was performed.
1845. August 27th No. 105.	Phebe Cryer	Daniel & Mary Anne	Lewis	Upton	Butcher	By G. D. Bowles Curate.
September 3rd No. 106.	John aged ten years	Samuel & Ann	Rossiter	Kingswood	Collier	By G. D. Bowles Curate
Sept 10th No. 107.	John	William & Sarah	Bush	Bitton	Labourer	G. D. Bowles Curate
Sept 17th No. 108.	Mary aged seven yrs	Richard & Hannah	Cains	Kingswood	Gardener	G. D. Bowles Curate
Sept 17th No. 109.	Sarah aged five yrs	Richard & Hannah	Cains	Kingswood	Gardener	G. D. Bowles Curate
Sept 17th No. 110.	Samuel aged fifteen yrs	Benjamin & Ann	Cains	Kingswood	Carrier	G. D. Bowles Curate
Sept 17th No. 111.	Joseph aged twelve yrs	Benjamin & Ann	Cains	Kingswood	Carrier	G. D. Bowles Curate
Sept 17th No. 112.	Sarah aged seventeen years	Benjamin & Ann	Cains	Kingswood	Carrier	G. D. Bowles Curate

George Caines was born around 1778, was sentenced to death for assault with intent to murder Constable Benjamin Curtis; this was commuted to transportation for life on 5 April 1815. George arrived in Australia aboard the vessel, Fanny, in 1816. He received a pardon on 28 November 1821 and lived out his working days as a butcher. He died in New South Wales, Australia in 1845 aged 67.

Francis Caines born on 19 December 1779, and was hanged on 12 September 1804 at Ilchester Somerset for his part in the robbery of a quantity of fine cloth.

Thomas Caines was born in 1785 in Bitton, Gloucestershire. He was convicted on the 16 August 1817 of stealing wheat and he was sentenced to transportation for seven years. After receiving his pardon he became an Innkeeper. He died on 9 September 1846 aged 61 in Cobbitty, Narellan, New South Wales.

Australian Convict Transportation Registers-other Fleets & Ships, 1791-1868

Thomas Caines

Benjamin Caines, was born in 1793, was condemned to death for the robbery of Sarah Prigg of Bitton. The judge pronounced that "execution should take place immediately and the body then hung in chains in a public place and left to rot" (this was changed to "just" hanging). He was buried on the 9 Sep 1817 in his home town of Bitton, Gloucestershire, in the same grave as his brother Francis. The burial register notes 'hanged'.

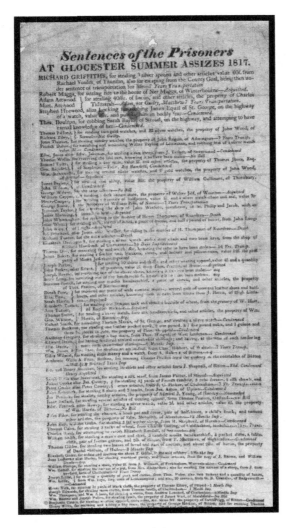

Benjamin Caines

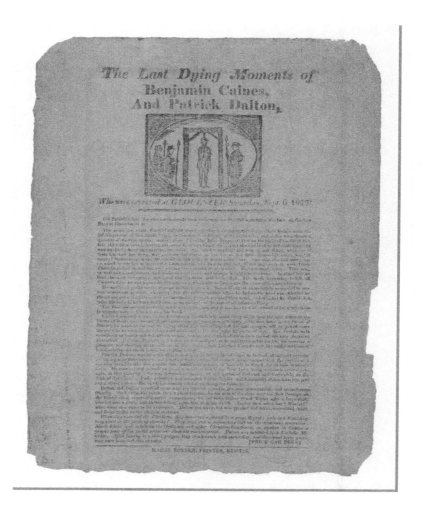

Samuel Caines was born in 1800 in Britton, Gloucestershire. On 28 March 1832, he was convicted of housebreaking and fowl stealing and sentenced to life transportation. He arrived in Australia on 6 January 1833 aboard the vessel, Mary. On 10 February 1840, he was given his ticket of freedom and worked as a hospital dispenser. He died in 1883, aged 83, in Liverpool, New South Wales, Australia, in the Liverpool Asylum for the Infirm and Destitute.

UK, Prison Hulk Registers and Letter Books, 1802-1849

The Caines family's youngest son, Joseph, was born in 1803 in Bitton. He was 16 years old when he was convicted of pocket-picking and was sentenced to seven years of transportation. However, the ship register dated November 1819 for Justitia, has this remark by his name 'Dead'. See below

Caines Joseph	Dead	Belongs to a Gang
Chipping John	NSW	Bad Char
Cotterel David	Sanym	Not Known befor
Craggs Henry	NSW	Bad Char.
Cohson Joseph	NSW	a thief from Childh

Benjamin and Ann's daughter Elizabeth had two illegitimate sons with Timothy Bush.

James and Francis baptism record

Their father Timothy Bush was, in March 1813, along with Thomas Wilmot and Joseph Willis, convicted of horse-stealing and sentenced to death. Their sentence was commuted to transportation for life.

Their oldest son James Caines, alias Bush, was sentenced to death along with Mark Whiting, for the murder of Isaac Garden; both were executed on 11 April 1825.

<table>
<tr><td colspan="2" style="text-align:center">12</td><td style="text-align:right">Reg.
1825.</td></tr>
</table>

17	*John Salmon*, aged 20, committed November 20, 1824, by Henry Borgh, Edw. Aldridge, and W. H. Hyett, Esqrs, charged upon the oaths of Samuel Webb, of the parish of Stroud, and others, with feloniously stealing, at the parish of Stroud aforesaid, on the 11th day of November instant, a quantity of linen and wearing apparel, the property of the said Samuel Webb.	62
18	*Jesse Beard*, aged 20, committed November 24, 1824, by Edw. Aldridge, Esq. charged with having, in company with three others, broken into the dwelling-house and shop of Thomas Smart, of the parish of Bisley, in the night of the 8th of this present month.	63
19	*Edward Hunt*, aged 18, committed November 24, 1824, by Edward Aldridge, Esq. charged on the oaths of six persons, with having sundry goods and household furniture stolen from them severally, and found in his house or possession at Bisley parish.	64
20	*James Churches* alias *James Jeffrys*, aged 25, committed November 29, 1824, by Henry Burgh, Esq. charged upon the oaths of Mary, the wife of Nathaniel Churches, of the parish of Painswick, and others, with feloniously and burglariously breaking and entering the dwelling-house of the said Nathaniel Churches, of the said parish of Painswick, in the night of the 27th day of November now instant, and stealing therein eighteen one-pound notes, and seven pounds in silver, and a pair of worsted stockings, the property of the said Nathaniel Churches.	69
21	*Joseph Lloyd* alias *Joseph Cottle*, aged 21, committed November 30, 1824, by Joseph Parker and John Haythorne, Esqrs. charged on the oath of John Glass, of the parish of Bitton, yeoman, on suspicion of having, at the parish aforesaid, in the night of Tuesday the 23d instant, feloniously broken open and entered his dairy, and stolen, taken, and carried away therefrom, ten green cheeses, value 2l. 10s. one chop of bacon, three pigs' hocks, a quantity of bread, meat, and other articles, value 20s. his property.	70

22	*Mark Whiting*, aged 24,	committed December 9, 1824, by Joseph Parker, Gabriel Goldney, Henry Brooke, John Haythorne, and John Savage, Esqrs. charged on the oath of George Haskins, of the parish of Bitton, yeoman, on suspicion of having, in the night of Saturday, the 27th day of November last, at the parish of Bitton aforesaid, feloniously assaulted, killed, and murdered, Isaac Garden.	82
23	*Isaac Britton*, aged 18,		83
24	*James Caines*, alias *Bush*, aged 20,		84
25	*Robert England*, aged 23,		85
26	*Samuel Peacock*, aged 23,		86
27	*Francis Britton*, aged 40,		87
28	*Thomas Wilmot*, aged 19,		88

Their second son Francis Caines Bush, aged 17, was on 12 August 1825, sentenced to death for Highway Robbery. The following day, his brother James was executed for murder.

The sentence was later commuted to transportation for life. He died on 27 April 1862, in Hobart, Hobart City, Tasmania, Australia. See below

Francis Caines / Bush 1821 prison record

Elizabeth had another son with a gentleman called George Groves who in 1822, was transported for life. Their son Thomas Caines/Groves befell the same fate as his father and was, on 11 August 1832, sentenced to transportation.

10

16 *Hannah Hignell*, aged 38, committed May 12, 1832, by Fiennes Trotman, Esq. charged on the oath of John Lewis, of the parish of Wick and Abson, farmer, on suspicion of having, at the parish of Bitton, feloniously received six score pounds of bacon, and four cheeses, of the value of 3*l*. 10*s*. 0*d*. the property of the said John Lewis, which had been stolen from him the said John Lewis, well knowing the same to have been stolen.

17 *William Wilkins*, aged 62, committed May 19, 1832, by H. W. Dyer, Esq. charged on the oath of George Tratman, of Dursley, farmer, on suspicion of having, on the 17th of May instant, feloniously stolen from a field in the parish of Cam, one lamb, the property of the said George Tratman.

18 *Thomas Cains* otherwise *Thomas Groves*, aged 19, committed May 22, 1832, by Gab. Goldney and Jos. Parker, Esqrs. charged on the oath of Robert Coole, of the parish of Bitton, labourer, on suspicion of having, on the 15th day of May instant, at the parish aforesaid, feloniously broken open his dwelling-house, and stolen two silver watches and other articles, value 8*l*. his property

Gloucestershire, England, prison records 1728-1914 Thomas Caines / Groves

Lydia Caines had two children with Jasper Wilmot before he was transported to Australia on 19 July 1818. Their son James Caines (Willmott) followed in his father's footsteps and was transported to Australia for seven years.

Benjamin Caines senior also had two nephews, both named Thomas Caines, and both were transported. He also had a half brother, Sampson Fry, who was also transported.

Thank you for reading our book, would you please consider leaving a small review on Amazon.

RESOURCES

All the documents and newspapers included in the book can be found at the following places.

www.capitalpunishmentuk.org/burning.html

Ancestry

https://www.ancestry.co.uk/

The National Library of Wales
https://newspapers.library.wales/

National Archives
https://discovery.nationalarchives.gov.uk/

https://commons.wikimedia.org/

Mary Blandy Photo

Harvard Library

https://hollis.harvard.edu/primo-explore/

THE LAST DYING MOMENTS OF BENJAMIN CAINES AND
PATRICK DALTON

Photos
Collation of Peter Coombes

REFERENCES'

Miss Mary Blandy's own Account of the Affair between Her and Mr Cranstoun (1751)

The Trial of Mary Blandy, Spinster: For the Murder of Her Father, Francis Blandy, Gent. At the Assizes Held at the County of Oxford, on Saturday the the29th of February 1752

John and James Rivington

The London Gazette: Part 1

Great Britain

By T Neuman

Celebrated Trials and Remarkable Cases of Criminal Jurisprudence from the Earliest Records to the Year 1825

By George Borrow (1825)

Dictionary of National Biography

Edited by Leslie Stephen and Sidney Lee (1890)

Gloucestershire Notes and Queries (1890)

William Phillimore and Watts Phillimore

Crown Cases Reserved For Consideration And Decided By The Twelve Judges Of England From The Year 1779 To The Year 1824.

By William Oldnall And Edward Ryan Of Lincoln's Inn, ESQRS, Barristers At Law. (1839)

By the same authors

Tales from the Tombstone

Buried Past: Tales from a Cheltenham Cemetery

Available from Amazon

In Paperback

On Kindle

And Kindle Unlimited

The Beautiful Churches Colouring Book

Available from Amazon

Printed in Great Britain
by Amazon

22442626R00138